MOTHERS IN MOURNING

A volume in the series

MYTH AND POETICS

edited by Gregory Nagy

A complete list of titles appears at the end of the book.

MOTHERS IN MOURNING

with the essay

Of Amnesty and Its Opposite

NICOLE LORAUX

Translated from the French by Corinne Pache

CORNELL UNIVERSITY PRESS

ITHACA AND LONDON

The publisher gratefully acknowledges the financial assistance of the French Ministry of Culture in defraying part of the cost of translation.

Originally published as *Les mères en deuil.* © Editions de Seuil, 1990. The final essay, "Of Amnesty and Its Opposite," was originally published as "De l'amnistie et de son contraire" in *Usages de l'oubli.* © Editions du Seuil, 1988.

First published 1998 by Cornell University Press.
First printing, Cornell Paperbacks, 1998.

Printed in the United States of America

Cornell University Press strives to utilize environmentally responsible suppliers and materials to the fullest extent possible in the publishing of its books. Such materials include vegetable-based, low-VOC inks and acid-free papers that are also either recycled, totally chlorine-free, or partly composed of nonwood fibers.

Library of Congress Cataloging-in-Publication Data

Loraux, Nicole.
Mothers in mourning : with the essay of amnesty and its opposite / Nicole Loraux ; translated from the French by Corinne Pache.
      p.   cm. — (Myth and poetics)
Includes index.
ISBN 0-8014-3090-9 (cloth : alk. paper). — ISBN 0-8014-8242-9 (pbk. : alk. paper)
   1. Mothers—Psychology.   2. Bereavement—Psychological aspects.   3. Mothers in literature.   4. Bereavement in literature.   I. Title.   II. Series.
HQ759.L59   1997
155.6'463—dc21   97-29264

Cloth printing   10   9   8   7   6   5   4   3   2   1
Paperback printing   10   9   8   7   6   5   4   3   2   1

the doating title of a mother

Richard III 4.4

Contents

Foreword

GREGORY NAGY

In the poetics of classical Athenian tragedy, it is conventional for a woman to react to the death of a loved one by singing a song of lamentation. The representations of these mythical laments as performed by mythical women are modeled, it is commonly assumed, on the real practice of lamentation as performed in all its myriad varieties by real women during the archaic and classical periods of ancient Greece. Such an assumption oversimplifies the mythology and the poetics of women's laments as represented by Athenian state theater. *Mothers in Mourning*, by Nicole Loraux, reexamines both the practice of women's lamentation and the representations of this practice, showing that the theatrical mimesis or "representation" of laments in tragedy is just as real, from the civic standpoint of the Athenian state, as is the practice of laments in "real life." When Athenian state theater represents a lament, this representation is far more than a mere fiction for the citizens who are the audience.

The idea that theater fictionalizes speech-acts such as laments goes back to Plato. In the *Laws*, for example, it is argued (658a–659c, 669b–670b) that theater appropriates real genres from real occasions and makes them make-believe. What turns the real into make-believe is mimesis or representation, inherent in theater. We may note that *eîdos*, a word used by Plato in the sense of "genre," is also used in the sense of "form" in his theory of forms. For Plato, theater merely represents genres, just as it merely represents reality.

As Loraux points out, Plato's condemnation of mimesis as a feature of theater in general and of tragedy in particular is specifically corre-lated in Book 3 of the *Republic* (395d–e) with the condemnation of imitating women's behavior, especially when it comes to lamenta-tion. For Plato the problem here is twofold: there is a danger not only in the representation but also in the reality that is being represented, namely, the real behavior of real women as they lament their dead.

For Plato, then, a lament in tragedy is a matter of mimesis or representation in the negative sense of an imitation, a fiction, where make-believe persons mourn for a make-believe dead person in a song that merely imitates a real occasion. From the standpoint of Athenian state theater, however, mimesis is not mere representation: rather, it is archetypal reenactment. That is, the songs of lamentation heard by the civic audience of Athenian state theater are taken to be archetypal, not derivative, in relation to the real-life laments of real-life people. Far from being an *imitation* of real-life genres, the drama-tized lament of Athenian state theater is taken to be a *model*.

We might expect such a model lament to follow professional rather than nonprofessional norms, and it is perhaps for this reason that the diction of tragedy does not distinguish, as does the diction of epic, between two types of lament—the professional *thrênos* and the non-professional *góos* (sung by next of kin). In the language of tragedy, they are treated as the same thing.

For the civic audience of Athenian state theater, the laments of tragedy are not only realistic: they are more real, even, than the laments sung by real women at real funerals. Moreover, unlike the potentially subversive laments sung by real women, these ultra-real laments heard by Athenian citizens in their state theater must be politically safe: after all, a lament staged by the state is presumably the self-expression of the state, as far as the Athenian audience is concerned.

And yet, things could go unexpectedly wrong, even in Athenian state theater. A notorious example is recorded by Herodotus (6.21):

in the year 492, the dramatist Phrynichus presented his Athenian audience with a tragedy about the capture of the Ionian city of Miletus by the Persians in 494. The dramatic representation of this holocaust, which marked the bitter end of the Ionian revolt, struck too close to home. The emotional impact on the audience—a veritable explosion of tears—led to such a political uproar that Phrynichus was fined one thousand drachmas as punishment for having "reminded" the Athenians "of their own misfortunes": that is, the Athenians' political self-identification as Ionians made them feel that the misfortunes of their fellow Ionians, their "kinsfolk," were really their own. Accordingly, any future performance of this tragedy about the capture of Miletus was interdicted by the state: tragedy must represent the grief of the Other, not of the Self. The Other must be distanced from the Self, whether in time (hence the appropriateness of myth in general) or in space (hence the appropriateness of Persia in Aeschylus's *Persians*). Emotionally, Ionian Miletus was not far enough away from Ionian Athens.

Such a permanent interdiction of a tragedy was tantamount to the banning of memory—that is, of certain kinds of memory. Here we confront the essence of the ancient Greek idea of *amnesty*, and Nicole Loraux has chosen this topic as the coda for her book, "Of Amnesty and Its Opposite."

Loraux argues that the ancient Greek mentality of amnesty is essential for understanding the mentality of lament. The obvious starting point is the affinity that exists between grief and anger. The emotions of grief, which are the wellspring of lament, spill over into emotions of anger, even rage. Ancient Greek literature is flooded with these spillovers, starting already with the *Iliad*: here the grief felt by Achilles over the slighting of his heroic honor undergoes a lethal metastasis into a form of anger so intense that it matches the cosmic dimensions of the rage manifested by Zeus himself in his divine reaction to human wrongdoing. The absolute quality of this cosmic anger, analyzed by Leonard Muellner in *The Anger of Achilles: Mênis in Early Greek Epic* (another book in the Myth and Poetics series), is analogous to the absolute nature of the epic expression *pénthos álaston*

'unforgettable grief'. The laments of women, of mothers in mourning, depend on the mentality of absolute grief: such grief, and the
absolute anger that goes with it, can never ever be erased from the
mind. Here we see the ultimate justification for revenge, for the spirit
of vendetta, for all the horrors of retaliation against earlier horrors.

Is there any social solution? Is there ever any absolution for absolute grief? Is there any way for society to solve the eternal problem of
endless cycles of retaliation, of ever new wrongs committed to avenge
the wrongs of the past? The relevance of these questions, as Loraux
suggests, surely transcends ancient Greek history. She mentions the
Dreyfus affair and the "Vichy syndrome"—and we may extend the
grim catalogue of grief ad infinitum, recalling such catastrophes as the
Jewish holocaust of the Third Reich and, more recently, the tragic
events in Palestine, Bosnia, Rwanda, and the list goes on.

In the year 403 before our era, the Athenian state presumed to
devise an absolute solution for absolute grief: it presumed to legislate
the erasure, even the absolution, of absolute grief. The word for this
social solution was *amnesty*, the formal civic act of selective non-
remembering. I say "selective" because this ancient Greek model
of amnesty did in fact systematically *remember* some essential things
while systematically *forgetting* other things deemed no longer essential
for the future. Amnesty is anything but value-free. The Athenian
amnesty of 403 simultaneously validated the restored democracy
and invalidated the overthrown oligarchy, which was thereafter to be
known forever as the régime of the Thirty Tyrants. The horrors of
the era of the Thirty were selectively remembered—and selectively
forgotten—but this selectivity was rendered absolute by the law.
Nearly a century earlier, in the year 492, the same kind of absolute
selectivity had been applied by the state to the Athenians' feelings of
grief over earlier horrors—in this case, the atrocities suffered by their
fellow Ionians.

In all these cases, the premier expression of grief was lament. Such
is the political as well as poetic power of women's lament, of mothers
in mourning.

Acknowledgments

These pages have a long history, but a combination of circumstances and friendly invitations has helped them take shape over just a few months.

After a first missed rendezvous (a conference about the mother in Delphi, which I could not attend), the opportunity to see these ideas through was given to me by Jacques-Gabriel Trilling, who asked me to present a talk in January 1989 at one of the meetings the Collège de Psychanalystes devoted to the subject of "the mother excluded from the political sphere."

To him I offer the warmest thanks, and I am also very grateful to all those who accompanied me on the path of mothers: Marie Moscovici and Yan Thomas, Laura Slatkin and Gregory Nagy, whose knowledge and friendship have been invaluable to me in the development of this text; the various audiences who generously discussed its main points, in Strasbourg (at the invitation of the association Le Maillon), at the École des Hautes Études en Sciences Sociales, and at Harvard University (on the occasion of a Helen Homans Gilbert Lecture) as well as at other universities in the United States; Françoise Peyrot and Olivier Bétourné, who welcomed me at Seuil; and, finally, Maurice Olender, who without hesitation offered a place to this book in the completely new Librairie du XXe siècle.

The Doating Title of a Mother

At the theater.

The play is *Richard III,* the performance is well under way.

The scene takes place in London, in front of the palace. Two women, two mothers, are seated on the ground. A third woman comes out of the shadows, and sits next to them . . . The scene is characteristically Shakespearean, whether we call it the great scene of queens, or, taking a Greek approach, whether we call it—and this would be my choice—the scene of mothers.[1]

Richard III, act 4, scene 4.

Two women, two mothers, after lamenting and uttering curses, sit down next to each other, on the ground. The first is the mother of a dead king and of a living king who owes his title solely to the murder of his elder brother; the second was the first king's wife, and she is also mourning her children, whom Richard put to death. Now the two women are sitting together on the ground.

Then, out of the shadows comes Queen Margaret, who was once also the wife of a murdered king and mother of an assassinated royal child. She speaks, and as she speaks, she sits down next to the other two.

---

[1] "La grande scène des reines," thus Henri Fluchère, p. 447 n. 4 in *Shakespeare: Oeuvres complètes* (Paris, 1959), 1: 1367.

> If ancient sorrow be most reverent,
> Give mine the benefit of seniory,
> And let my griefs frown on the upper hand.
> If sorrow can admit society, [*Sitting down with them*]
> Tell o'er your woes again by viewing mine.
>
> (*Richard III* 4.4.35–39)

Three queens, three mothers, sitting on the ground, next to one another. On the ground—this once faithful English ground that now knows no law—is the resting place that the Duchess of York had been yearning for, the resting place that since the death of a son killed by a son, she has forever lost, so that her entire being rejects the very notion of it ("Rest thy unrest," she exhorts herself). This is a dubious resting place, a "melancholy seat," comments her daughter-in-law, who, in place of her own longing for rest, has substituted a desire for death: may not the earth become her grave? And Queen Elizabeth sits down in her turn, and soon Queen Margaret joins her. "Ah, who hath any cause to mourn but we?" says Elizabeth to her husband's mother. Margaret answers by demanding the place of honor for her sorrow. It is as if sitting on the ground were a symbol that the path of dejection had been pursued to its very end. This is the dejection of kings stripped of their kingdoms, and of queens whose sons have been killed.[2] Then, if she does not deny herself the timeless pleasure of free association, a Greek-minded reader may think of prostrate Demeter, sitting under an olive tree, engrossed in her lost daughter's dereliction; and in the sorrow of queens, as in that of goddesses, she may hear the mourning of mothers.[3]

---

[2] See *Richard II* 3.2.155–56 (King Richard: "For God's sake, let us sit upon the ground and tell sad stories of the death of kings").

[3] See *Homeric Hymn to Demeter* 98 and 197, with commentary on line 197 by N. J. Richardson, *The Homeric Hymn to Demeter* (Oxford, 1974); see also Euripides *Helen* 1325–26 (in her grief, the Great Mother throws herself on snowy rocks). With Richardson, we will evoke the day of the Thesmophoria when, fasting (*nēsteía*), Athenian women are "'seated on the ground' in the same prostrate position as that adopted by Demeter when Persephone was separated from her" (M. Detienne, *The*

In act 2, the Duchess declares to a widow and orphans—her son Edward's wife, her son Clarence's children—"Alas, I am the mother of these griefs! Their woes are parcell'd, mine are general."[4] Richard's mother is the mother of griefs insofar as her womb produced a monster. When she says her woes are "general" it is a way of confessing that the widow and the orphans owe their sad state to Richard III, and thus to her, who curses her womb throughout the drama for having given shelter to such a son. But the same words may also mean that a mother's sorrow is general in the sense that it is generic, a general sorrow that contains all mourning within itself.

A mother has given birth to mourning. Does a mother's mourning give birth to all the sorrows of her progeny?

In *Richard III*, no woman escapes the hold of the fertility of the maternal motif. For instance, at the beginning of act 4, Edward's sons await the hangman's noose in front of the Tower of London. Elizabeth and the Duchess claim their right to see their children: "I am their mother; who shall bar me from them?" "I am their father's mother; I will see them." But it is another woman's words that capture our attention, those of hapless Anne, widow of Margaret's son, and Richard's wife: "Their aunt I am in law, in love their mother." But it is doubtful whether such a statement is admissible in *Richard III*; it is belied by the facts (while the women are speaking, the children are being killed), and nothing in the drama's internal logic ensures that love is enough to make a mother.

After three more scenes, the queens meet. Three women again, with the difference that Margaret replaces Anne (who has gone to meet her fate), and resentment supplants love. This all takes place against a background of hate and complicity that is impossible to disentangle. Hate is born between Margaret and the other two women from this long carnage, euphemistically called war—a war in the

---

Gardens of Adonis [Princeton, 1977], 80). Yet in the *Hymn* Demeter's sitting position is a way for the goddess to renew her sorrow, as M. Arthur notes in "Politics and Pomegranates: An Interpretation of the *Homeric Hymn to Demeter*," *Arethusa* 10 (1977): 20.

  [4] *Richard III* 2.2.80–81.

family, which the Greeks themselves understood as the ultimate civil war—which sets York against Lancaster and Lancaster against York. And, as if to make the hate go deeper, the same names (Richard, Edward) recur, from one branch to the other, to designate the victims and the murderers, all fathers, sons, brothers, cousins—all are kings, kings' sons, or kings-to-be. Margaret's husband killed or had killed the Duchess's husband and one of her sons; the Duchess's eldest son, Edward, overthrew the king, whom Richard murdered just as he had murdered his son; then Richard killed his brother. And this creates a sinister funereal accounting among the mothers, even more so since within one of the rival branches itself there exists a bitter competition among the queens that turns into a mourning contest.[5] But it is Margaret, filled with a relentless desire for revenge, who manifests the full measure of pure hatred:

> I had an Edward, till a Richard kill'd him;
> I had a Henry, till a Richard kill'd him:
> [*To Queen Elizabeth*]
> Thou hadst an Edward, till a Richard kill'd him;
> Thou hadst a Richard, till a Richard kill'd him.

To which, the Duchess answers:

> I had a Richard too, and thou didst kill him;
> I had a Rutland too, thou holp'st to kill him.
>
> (*Richard III* 4.4.40–45)

Thus the hatred is all the more fierce in that it feeds on sameness. But Margaret's greatness lies in the Queen-Erinys's knowledge that there is a sort of dreadful complicity or even better—this is her word—a "society" among mourning mothers. She once hated Elizabeth; now for a moment she can be her ally, since the same Richard, in order to become Richard III, is responsible for both women's woes; thus Elizabeth asks Margaret for lessons in hate against her enemies. Margaret

---

[5] See, for example, act 2, scene 2 (the Duchess, Queen Elizabeth).

can share her hateful mourning even with the Duchess, the mother of a man the old queen calls the "carnal cur," since Richard has made his mother "pew-fellow with others' moans!" The ancient Greeks made the god of war (of murder) a harsh judge; Richard is the bloody reconciliator among enemy mothers . . .

We especially remember this lesson for Elizabeth from Queen Margaret, a reminder to transform mourning into curse at every instant,

> Forbear to sleep the night, and fast the day;
> Compare dead happiness with living woe;
> Think that thy babes were fairer than they were,
> And he that slew them fouler than he is:
> Bettering thy loss makes the bad-causer worse:
> Revolving this will teach thee how to curse.
>
> (*Richard III* 4.4.118–23)

Mourning leads to cursing: this is the lesson given to the gentle Elizabeth, but which we could well imagine given by a Greek mother from the depth of her grief, except that in Greek tragedy a mother does not need to learn how to hate: the ordeal teaches her.

But we are not finished with this scene from *Richard III*, in which Shakespeare relentlessly amplifies the grief of being a mother. The greatest sorrow is perhaps that of the Duchess of York, because she hates her son. She hates him because he killed her two other sons, and for her, as for Margaret, there is hate in mourning. And she hates him from the start, because he, her son, was born malformed, and because from the first hour, the sight of Richard was distressing to her. As soon as Margaret leaves, Richard arrives and stumbles against his mother's imprecations. It is an amazing moment, when each understands the other's hate. One exchange is enough to suggest it:

Duchess.
> Thou cam'st on earth to make the earth my hell.

> .   .   .   .

King Richard.

> If I be so disgracious in your eye,
> Let me march on, and not offend you, madam.
>
> *(Richard III* 4.4.167, 178–79)

The mother's last word is to curse her son for all time. Freud could have made much of this curse, if, as some believe, he had practiced applied psychoanalysis:[6] we need only evoke the next-to-last scene of the play, in which the forlorn king attempts to persuade himself, against his growing self-hate, that "Richard loves Richard," before recognizing that this cannot be true, since "there is no creature loves me."[7] Throughout the long night, the ghosts of his victims have come to him to curse him, to reiterate the first malediction, which his own mother, standing before him, threw in his face.

Richard III is about power and its monstrosity, they say. But it is also about mothers, mourning, and hatred, which awakens a Greek echo. With, nonetheless, its characteristically Shakespearean dimension: that the relationship of the wives and mothers to their husbands and sons is a relationship to power itself. When they weep over their dead spouses or killed sons, they lament not so much the dead body of a kinsman as the king and the power that has been lost, and the name that has been obliterated.

During a performance of the drama, the shock felt at seeing and listening to the scene of the queens stirred in me—in the Hellenist in

---

[6] In "Some Character-Types Met with in Psychoanalytic Work," *The Standard Edition of the Complete Psychological Works of Sigmund Freud,* trans. James Strachey (London, 1957), 14:314, Freud, analyzing Richard of Gloucester's opening monologue ("What the soliloquy thus means is: 'Nature has done me a grievous wrong in denying me the beauty of form which wins human love. Life owes me reparation for this.'"), speaks only of nature, and not of the mother. On this point, he is faithful to the text, which evokes only "dissembling nature." This also suits him perfectly, since he saves the wrong inflicted by the mother for the reproaches of the daughter against the one who caused her to be born a woman.

[7] *Richard III* 5.3.183, 200.

me—a very ancient desire to understand what it is that, in the Greek context, makes the mourning of mothers a challenge to political life as it is defined by the city-state. The time has come to offer at least a few paths by which to approach this question: be it for the delights afforded by Shakespeare or through fidelity to a dramatic performance or because of the conviction that there is fruitfulness to be found in digression, I propose to begin with the hiatus of this false start. It is also true that for us, who cannot directly feel Greek, Shakespeare may well be the necessary locus for any investigation of dramatic passion. Because, whether ironically abrasive or secretly nostalgic, the word *passion* is again Richard's word, when, in the same scene he evokes "the doating title of a mother."[8]

But what happens to passion in the city-state?

---

[8] *Richard III* 4.4.300. We should note that *doat* (or *dote*) has the double meaning "to love passionately" and "to drivel," *doting* meaning, then, either "who loves passionately" or "senile": all the ambivalence—Richard's, to be sure; that of the maternal figure, perhaps—is found in this word.

Measures against Feminine Excess

Passion in the city-state?

Páthos affecting the citizens? Danger.

Sometimes, the excesses of *páthos* are unpredictable: then, for having failed to contain them in advance, we carefully date them, and we entrust their negative imprints to civic memory as a warning for the future. Thus it is that Herodotus can easily obtain from the Athenians the tale of that day on which the tragedy about the defeat of Miletus gushes out of the orchestra and floods the seats until the whole theater is in tears. There was a great risk that the Athenians would start doubting their policy toward their sister-cities. Hence comes the fine imposed on Phrynichus and the ban on the performance of his play: for the edification of future citizens, or for the use of future investigators. But the alert is over, and the measures taken are proven effective: no other tragedian will offer the Athenians such an unmediated reflection of disturbing current events.[1]

Usually *páthos* is as recurrent and predictable as the unavoidable events that shape human time; thus the city, as a well-organized collectivity, enacts a series of laws and regulations against the danger

---

[1] This anecdote, told by Herodotus (6.21), is analyzed in greater detail below in N. Loraux, "Of Amnesty and Its Opposite."

of unbridled passion. And it is under this heading that we should consider the question of mourning and of the practices that shape and limit it, though without forgetting what is unmanageable in it, what characteristically resists all strategy.

In other words, we should consider what the Greek city makes of mourning, and what it does not want to make of it.

What the city makes of it is not difficult to make out: we can mention and study—we do mention, study—rituals with which the civic community attempts to circumscribe the *páthos* of mourning.[2] If we are more interested in what the city rejects, as is the case here, we should seek what the city fears. Because, with all due respect to functionalist discourse, which assumes that with appropriate treatment loss is virtually eliminated without a trace (as if loss were not the presence of what weighs the most heavily),[3] nothing ever ensures that funeral rites will be enough to exorcise the fascination of loss—this "pleasure of tears" and of suspended time that epic evokes without pretense, and that threatens the political sphere in its positivity. Hence the rejection of memory when it tries to be guardian of rifts and breaches: the city wants to live and perpetuate itself without breaks, and its citizens must not wear themselves out with crying. Then, rejected by both the Ceramicus and the Agora—both from the official burying ground and from political space—the unmanageable remnant flows back to the theater, *intra muros,* but is kept away from the civic self;[4] representations of mourning, of its greatness and its perplexities, fill tragedy, because the tragic genre dramatizes the essential exclusions the city has instituted for the citizens' use. What is true of mourning is true of women, and it is only natural that Plato, in book

---

[2] See D. Kurtz and J. Boardman, *Greek Burial Customs* (London, 1971), 142–61 passim; and E. De Martino, *Morte e pianto rituale nel mondo antico* (Turin, 1958), 195–222 (on ritual as a way of ordering grief).

[3] See, for example, some of Louis Vincent-Thomas's formulations, in T. Nathan, ed., "Rituels de deuil, travail du deuil," *Nouvelle revue d'ethnopsychiatrie* 10 (1988), especially the "quatrième de couverture," in which an observation that was once subtle and open becomes more rigid.

[4] Loraux, "Of Amnesty and Its Opposite."

3 of the *Republic*, defining the ban on *mímēsis* (thus on theater, and especially on tragedy), specifies that guardians are prohibited from imitating women, "being men";[5] and we find surrender to grief and lamentation among the feminine forms of behavior that are not to be imitated.[6] Whoever wants to discuss women and mourning in the city cannot bypass Athenian tragedy.

Mourning, women . . . if we decide to end the list of prohibitions here, it is because the conjunction between mourning and women is not an accident. Already in the archaic city, the lament of mourning is feminine, and as Archilochus's famous poem exhorts, it must be banished.[7] The object of the prohibition is the potential threat that women's mourning constitutes for civic order—its expression not being pleonastic in itself, when considered from a citizen's point of view it is a pleonasm.

A threat to be contained, but also to be fantasized about. And we may ask: is it contained so that we may fantasize about it in complete safety? Which suggests that we should analyze the manipulations and processes of thought that the civic community uses to get rid of the threat without completely freeing itself from it, in ritual practice just as in the politics of myth.

First to mourn—in tragedy as in the funeral regulations that identify those women whose presence will be tolerated at funerals—first to moan and first to provoke the tears of those around them, in the first row of mourning women, mothers will be particularly in evidence. The city's laws address citizens' wives or goddesses identified with their grief, mythical queens or generic figures. A generally Greek political discourse takes up each and every one of them, and, to

---

[5] On the exclusion of women as "one of the motors of tragic action" ("un des moteurs de l'action tragique"), see P. Vidal-Naquet, *Tragédies* (Paris, 1982), 30–31 (preface to Aeschylus).

[6] Plato *Republic* 3.395d–e. We should note that the strongest proscription is against the woman "sick or in love or in labor" (Phaedra, or Auge, who gives birth in a temple); as for the woman who competes with the gods and boasts of her own happiness and the one who surrenders to lamentation, they are identical with Niobe, at two different stages of her story.

[7] Archilochus frag. 13 West.

understand it, we shall not abstain from using any kind of documents, even those that—in their comparative differentness—pertain to Roman mothers, often exemplary. This, of course, makes for an incongruous project and presupposes respect for differences and recourse to extremely diverse strategies. I accept the risk, since the challenge is to track, in what is dissimilar, a similar point of view toward the question of sex and politics.

We should note—if only this once—that Athenian practice can be described in short as "normal" as regards mothers, to the degree that we would call it Greek practice were it not for the inhumanly heroic Spartan mothers. It is in Athens, in any case, that the civic ideology of maternity is best represented. A woman can accomplish her *télos* (her goal) only in giving birth, and although there is no female citizenship, motherhood nonetheless counts as a civic activity. By giving birth, citizens' wives assure their husbands perpetuation of their descent and name—without their intervention, there would be no patronymic—and thus they guarantee the continuation of the city. It is difficult sometimes not to entertain the idea that by giving birth to sons (since in the official orthodoxy, only male children are of any account) women bear sons for the city. If we were to forget that Aristophanes' comedy exists primarily to produce laughter, it would be tempting to believe that there existed a female political discourse entirely based on the pride of being a mother. Motherhood is in itself a form of taxation ("I pay my taxes by contributing men [*ándras*]"),[8] and because of this women can contend, on the comic stage, that when they celebrate the civic festival of the Thesmophoria:

> We, women, could rightly blame
> men for many things, and for one most enormous.
> For it is necessary, if one of us gives birth
> to a man useful to the city (*ándra khrēstón*),[9]
> a taxiarch, or a general, that she should obtain some honor,

[8] Aristophanes *Lysistrata* 651.
[9] *Khrēstós* characterizes the citizen as he fulfills his duties; conversely, *ákhrēstos* or *akhreíos* suggests a uselessness that is detrimental to the citizenry.

and be given the front seat at the Stenia or the Scira
or at any other festival we celebrate.

(Aristophanes Thesmophoriazusae 830–35)

And the unlikely programme of the women's government, or rather
of the mothers', is also described:

> Let us then, O men, hand the city over to them
> without delay. . . . Let us consider this only,
> first, that, being mothers (prôton oûsai mētéres),
> they will be eager to save the soldiers.
> Then, as for food, who will supply it better
> than the one who gave birth (tês tekoúsēs)?

(Aristophanes Ecclesiazusae 229–35)

If the citizen is a soldier by definition, it is the mothers' burden-
some task to "doubly endure war, first by giving birth, then by sending our sons away as soldiers" (tekoûsai, ekpémpsasai paîdas hoplítas).[10]
But female orators in comedy carefully omit one detail, which, although less ideological, is nevertheless so commonplace that it serves
as a topos: as they send their sons to war, women cry. A tragic queen—
Praxithea, in Euripides' Erechtheus—recalls this and hastens to add
that she hates women who prefer life to honor for their sons.[11] It is
true that Praxithea is an extremist of civic motherhood, an "Athenian" more than a mother (I would gladly call her a mother first if she
did not wrap herself in the autochthonous ideal), and more Spartan
than Athenian. Spartan mothers are supposed to offer their shield to
their sons going to war, and to exhort them to come back "with it or
on it." If Praxithea had had sons, she would have armed them with
spears without fearing their deaths, and, just as a Lacedaemonian
woman, she would no doubt have wept over their cowardice rather

---

[10] Lysistrata 589–90. Giving birth is itself a kind of military feat: see N. Loraux,
The Experiences of Tiresias (Princeton, 1995), 23–30.

[11] Fragment quoted by Lycurgus (Against Leocrates 100.29–31, in the midst of a
patriotic medley; see the edition of P. Carrara, Euripide, Eretteo [Florence, 1977],
frag. 10).

than their patriotic deaths.[12] Alone in reigning over their men, Spartan mothers think they owe this exceptional status to the fact that they alone "give birth to men." Even if she exhibits quiet joy when her sons die, saying that they belonged to Lacedaemonia as much as to herself,[13] the Spartan mother does not go so far as to deny the maternal bond by virtue of which, for each and every one of them, he was "mine." Praxithea, however, has had, as she puts it, *only* daughters, and she must sacrifice one of them for the city; transgressing all norms, and first and foremost those of her sex, elated with a very personal fanatical sense of citizenship that she pushes to the limits of deceit, she does not content herself with offering her daughter but declares she freely gives this daughter "who is mine only by birth" (*ouk emền plền ề phúsei*);[14] hence it follows that the Athenian queen is more than woman, more than Athenian, more even than honorific Spartan, but less than mother. She is neither the paradigm of the "strength of women" nor a happy example of the "autochthonous mother."[15]

On stage, Athenian citizens could still recognize their women in the proud arguers of Aristophanes; on the other hand, they very probably put Praxithea in the category of maximum excess. It follows

[12] This is the mild version of a patriotic behavior that can reach the extremes of fanaticism: Plutarch tells the story of the Spartan mother who sees her son come back alone from a defeat in which all the others died, and kills him with a tile, just as women kill the enemy by throwing tiles during a *stásis* (insurrection) (*Moralia* 241b; cf. 240a and 241a). After the severe defeat at Leuctra, Spartan women showed their valor, according to Plutarch (*Moralia* 241c, 242a; *Agesilaus* 30.7); Xenophon's less edifying account, on the other hand, mentions the injunction to them "not to lament and to bear their sorrow in silence" (*Hellenica* 6.4.16)—symbolizing the great difference between reality and legend.

[13] *Moralia* 241a: *kaì emòn kaì Lakedaimónion.*

[14] Strange depreciation of what is *phúsei* (by nature or by birth), unless there is some opposition between a biological *phúsis* and an autochthonous *phúsis* (line 8); we can appreciate Lycurgus's observation that this woman prefers her country against nature (*phúsei*), which requires that women love their children (*génos philóteknon*).

[15] Contra Marcel Detienne, in G. Sissa and M. Detienne, *La vie quotidienne des dieux grecs* (Paris, 1989), chap. 14 and p. 241. "Rectifier" of the foundations of Athens, Praxithea, like Creusa in Euripides' *Ion*, albeit in a different mode, crystallizes the tragic paradoxes of autochthony when it is borne by a woman.

that mothers' tears are not only a topos, but reality itself, anterior to any ideological proclamation and, as if by nature, untouched.

What about reality itself? Let us leave the theater and its meaningful fictions, and go to the Ceramicus cemetery, where public funerals of the Athenians who died for the city are held. What behavior, exactly, are mothers allowed to adopt when their citizen-sons actually perish for Athens?

It would be better to ask what role is assigned to them, and to answer straight off that the role of mothers is, in such circumstances, to be absent.

There is Thucydides' description of the ceremony in book 2 of the *Peloponnesian War,* given rhythm by the three beats required by the exposition (*próthesis*), the procession (*ekphorá*), and the burial (*táphos*). About the *próthesis,* we learn little, and nothing indicates a feminine presence in the *ekphorá;* thus it is only in extremis that "women relatives are standing by the grave, lamenting."[16] Everything suggests that there are only men among the "volunteers," the citizens and foreigners who accompany the procession. If women walk alongside the men, Thucydides wants to hear nothing of it—which, in the text, amounts to the same thing—because female lamentations have no place in Athenian streets. Women will appear later, at the cemetery, the only place where their lamentations are allowed, albeit in a codified form. Women? More exactly, "some women, the relatives, are there" (*gunaîkes páreisin, hai prosékousai*). This is a rather restricted group, then, in which mothers are tacitly included without deserving any special mention. When it comes to mothers, discretion is required.

The funeral oration also confirms this, for Pericles says nothing about mothers. No doubt they would have a right to be included in the plural "parents" (*toùs tônde tokéas*). The statement that one must "be strong with the hope of other children when still of age to have

[16] Thucydides 2.34.4. From this point of view, we will contrast the Athenian practice with the Spartan mourning ceremonies for the death of a king, in which women participate alongside the men (Herodotus 6.58).

them" seems to evoke more specifically women, who are biologically limited by their age. But, faithful to its purely political logic, the funeral oration soon denies these commonsense assumptions: if there is a need to have children ready to face dangers, it is because it is necessary to ensure a succession. Only then will they be able to "participate in deliberations justly and equally." Mothers have disappeared, assuming that they ever were included in the group of "parents,"[17] and they will not be included in the category "women," which Pericles reserves for widows. Once more, it is all about *ándres,* their "age," whether they are good for war and for fathering children or marked because of their uselessness (*tò akhreîon tês hēlikías*), typical of the citizen described by Aristotle as "incomplete."[18]

Not a word, then, has been said about mothers: it is true that by speaking of the new children who will bring forgetfulness of the dead ones,[19] he could not decently be addressing them, whom Greek tradition unanimously describes as the keepers of memory.

The same is true of the *epitáphios* of the *Menexenus,* even though there are many allusions to childbearing throughout the speech, as if to place the funeral oration outside its mandatory references.[20] As soon, however, as the exhortation addresses the living, mothers fade

[17] Which is not self-evident if, like Apollo in the *Eumenides* (658–61), Thucydides refuses to give the title *tokeús* 'procreator' to mothers. Yan Thomas has pointed out to me that the same is true of *parens,* which has been transformed from the vocabulary of childbirth for the benefit of fathers; see Thomas's article "Le ventre, corps maternel, droit paternel," *Le genre humain* 14 (1986): 213. It is interesting to note that there are five occurrences of *mếtēr* in Thucydides books 1 and 2 (three of which refer to Alcmaeon, who kills his mother), against nine of *patếr* and twenty-four of *patéres.*

[18] Thucydides 2.44.1 (*tokéas*), 2.44.3 (age and deliberation), 2.44.4 (*tò akhreîon tês hēlikías*). On *akhreîon,* see Thucydides 2.40.2 and N. Loraux, *The Invention of Athens* (Cambridge, 1986), 408 n. 17.

[19] Thucydides 2.44.3.

[20] Exordium: exhortations and consolation addressed to *patéras kaì mētéras* (*Menexenus* 236e); autochthony: dead Athenians, fed not by a stepmother but by a true mother, will rest in the "intimate places" of the one who gave birth to them, nourished, and welcomed them (237b–c); giving birth and feeding one's child: women imitate earth (237e–238a); democracy: Athenians are all brothers from the same mother, and thus they are all equal (239a).

out. There are two more occurrences of the pair "fathers and mothers,"[21] and already the figure of the all-benevolent city comes into
view. The noun for "city" is feminine, but as regards those in mourning, it undertakes exclusively male roles, starting with that of father,
which it assumes for orphans.[22] In the *Menexenus,* it is in this capacity
that it takes up the dead men's role and ensures the education (*paideía*)
of their children, while with regard to "nourishment"—or rather
"rearing" (*trophḗ*)—it is a nourisher only in addition (*sunektréphei*),
against the tradition that, from Thucydides to Aeschines, requires that
the care and civic honoring of war orphans be included in *tréphein.*[23]
This follows the requirements of the paternal figure, which Plato
associates with *paideía,* while the mother is all "nourishment."[24]

   Paideía / trophḗ: education vs. feeding-rearing. This Platonic opposition introduces our first Roman detour, in which Rome, to be sure,
is seen from Greece. We have the example of Coriolanus, an only son
and an orphan brought up by his mother. A great warrior, and mortal
enemy of the people, he is banished from the city he has betrayed,
until he is brought back at last (and to his own demise) to a more civic
attitude by his mother's tears. Dionysius of Halicarnassus and Plutarch tell the story as an integral part of ancient Roman history, but
since he wrote people's lives, Plutarch is the only one to anchor his
account in the childhood of a mother's son.[25] The tone is given at
the outset, in the first chapter: fatherless, brought up by his mother
(*trapheìs hupò mētrí*), Gaius Marcius bears witness that "a nature gen-

---

[21] *Menexenus* 247c and 248b; see also 249e.

[22] *Menexenus* 249a: *en patròs skhḗmati katastásas autoís.*

[23] I could also translate this word as "maintenance," since the usual meaning of
trophḗ is "nourishment" of children, but I also take into account its original meaning
"to rear," "to grow," studied by P. Demont, "Remarques sur le sens de *tréphō,*" *Revue
des études grecques* 91 (1978): 358–84. At 248d, *paideúein* is the role of the father.
Sunektréphei: 249a. On the tradition of the *trophḗ* of orphans see Thucydides 2.46.1;
Lysias *Against Theozotides* 2; Aeschines *Against Ctesiphon* 154.

[24] As the "mother" of Athenians, the Attic land assumes a nourishing function,
but with regard to *paideía* (238b5), she introduces teachers, who are the gods.

[25] This is, incidentally, a Roman theme. See F. Dupont, *La vie quotidienne du
citoyen romain sous la République* (Paris, 1989), 142–45.

erous and good, when it lacks education (*paideía*), produces a medley of excellent and hateful fruits." A father's *paideía* would have extracted the best from his strong character and great energy. Should we, then, see the relentless anger and inflexible obstinacy that made him unaccommodating (*oud' euhármoston*) as maternal legacies? Endowed with three of the cardinal virtues, Coriolanus nevertheless lacks *sōphrosúnē* (moderation), the only virtue that Greek thought agrees to ascribe to women, though not without some doubts and reservations. But under the circumstances, the mother could give nothing to her beloved son; male *sōphrosúnē* is civic, completely different from the chaste female *sōphrosúnē*. Now Coriolanus—because he lacked a father—is unable to take part in reciprocal relationships with his fellow citizens (*politikaì homilíai*). Plutarch even comments that education alone teaches moderation and the rejection of excess. From the mother to her son, and from the son to his mother, the relationship is thus distorted: glory, the crowning of courage, is for the son only a way of delighting his mother, and she, hearing him being praised, weeps (already), but for joy. To be sure, Coriolanus does not know what a father is, certain as he feels that he owes "to his mother the part of gratitude that was due to his father."[26] Thus, whatever she herself says, he puts his mother first, before even his country—this fatherland—for which Plutarch blames him: he would have done better certainly "not to spare his fatherland because of his mother, but his mother together with his fatherland; because his mother and his wife are just parts of the city he was attacking." Yielding to Volumnia's tears, not for an instant does he aim at anything other than "to please" his mother.[27] Warped by an excess of *trophḗ*, Coriolanus is a citizen against nature.[28]

I close this parenthesis for the time being. We shall, however, meet again with Coriolanus's mother and her effective tears. At all events,

[26] Plutarch *Coriolanus* 4.5

[27] Plutarch *Coriolanus* 33.9, 35.4, 36.3 (and passim in Volumnia's speech); also 36.5 (Coriolanus's answer is "I am conquered by you alone"). For Plutarch's opinion, see 43.4–5.

[28] See N. Loraux, "Citoyen contre nature," *Théâtre public* 49 (1983): 42–45.

this very private story brings us back to the mourning of mothers in the private burial ceremonies of the Greek cities.

Laws exist to delimit the bounds of mourning. Let us consider these laws, usually considered typical of the archaic period because we always want to attribute them to the great lawgivers of that era, and because they supposedly attempt to curtail the powers of the aristocracy by every means available (although actual documents hardly confirm this presupposition, since they date from the end of the fifth century, or even from the fourth and third centuries B.C.).[29]

By confining private funerals within extremely strict limits, the city regulates mourning and the role played by women in the context of mourning. This also suggests that the city regulates mourning, and thus it regulates women. Or perhaps we should say that it regulates women, and thus mourning, so strongly does the reciprocal relation between women and mourning assert itself in those texts. Yet we first have to recognize this "obvious fact," the significance of which few commentators care to acknowledge.

Antiaristocratic measures aimed at curbing luxury and expenses: such is the accepted interpretation of these civic funeral laws (*nómoi*), and this is more than likely partially correct.[30] Thus it is that historians

[29] This is the received opinion—given the constraints of a city undergoing democratization—and if the documents are later, we are tempted to see them as "reformulations" of earlier laws; see M. Alexiou, *The Ritual Lament in Greek Tradition* (Cambridge, 1974), 15–16. For a similar, though more nuanced, position, see C. Ampolo, "Il lusso funerario e la città arcaica," *Annali dell' Istituto orientale di Napoli* 6 (1984): 92–94. We should not necessarily eliminate the hypothesis that laws have been retrospectively attributed to ancient lawgivers. See F. Jacoby's commentary on Philochorus fragment 65 (essentially, Athenian legislation on *gunaikonómoi* is to be dated around the time of the orator Lycurgus or Demetrios of Phaleron).

[30] This is an accepted notion among the ancients: see the purely sumptuary interpretation offered by Diodorus (11.38) of the Syracusan legislation in the time of Gelon. The best treatment of the question of luxury is that of C. Ampolo, who rightly insists that "limitation of luxury and regulation of rituals go together" ("Il lusso funerario," 95); see also C. Ampolo, "Il lusso nelle società arcaiche: Note preliminari sulla posizione del problema," *Opus* 3 (1984): 469–76; Alexiou, *Ritual Lament,* 18.

of the ancient world are often eager to relate everything that concerns women to this general reading, because, as they think, it is reasonable for cities irresistibly set on the path of "democratization" to restrict the role of noblewomen—and at the same time of all women—in those ceremonies in which they play an important part. There are certainly good reasons for such a discourse; there are also some more debatable ones. It is perfectly reasonable to decide to treat mourning regulations as an indivisible whole, because in the Greece of city-states, funeral rites—Herodotus's *History* bears witness to this—constitute a conspicuous criterion of "Greekness"; if we link a law limiting the display of feminine grief to a general movement of democratization, the reasoning, were it formulated, could be supported, since it is true that in ancient Greece women are even farther removed from the political sphere under democratic regimes than under other constitutions.

I confess, however, that I am not satisfied by such narrowly historicizing readings, because they deliberately ignore what we will call, by deference to Greek convention, the "soul of the city."[31] Those readings generally do not even begin to solve the problems (difficult, but—I wager—necessary, at least as working hypotheses) that we encounter when we treat the city as a subject. To set on such a path, we are compelled to broaden the perspective and to give more attention generally to the vigilant coherence with which cities defend the political sphere against behaviors and emotions that threaten its harmony. Mourning is among those, and it may even be a privileged example: consider the central place of the prohibition concerning the *thrênos* (lamentation) in the funeral oration, or, as concerns memory that is enamoured of revenge, consider what takes place in the Greek procedure for amnesty.[32] I would also like to suggest that mourning, perceived as essentially feminine, must be thrust aside by ascribing to women, and especially to mothers, as limited a role as possible, since

[31] N. Loraux, "L'âme de la cité: Réflexions sur une *psychè* politique," *L'écrit du temps* 14/15 (1987): 35–54.

[32] *Thrênos:* Loraux, *Invention of Athens,* 44–50; amnesty: Loraux, "Amnesty and Its Opposite."

in these laws—just as, in many respects, in the political thought of Aristotle—the main concern is to watch over the stability of the city without respite.[33]

Before we even begin to consider feminine behavior, it is clear that the same prescriptions are found from one funeral law to the next, even when we consider two texts as dissimilar as a philosophical fiction and an actual law:[34] both the *thrênos* and any kind of crying outside the house are prohibited, and, generally, great attention is given to the particulars of the *ekphorá*.[35] Let us consider at greater length what concerns women, from Solon—since unquestionably everything must start with a great lawgiver—to a law from Ceos and then a later one from Gambreion in Asia Minor.[36]

According to Plutarch, Solon wanted to check women's disorderliness and license. He thus prohibited them from lacerating their skin (by which mourning women attempted to reproduce on their own cut-up bodies the injury done by death to the corpse), from using *thrênoi* in verse, and from lamenting any other dead. In the fifth century B.C., after enacting strict sumptuary restrictions, the city of Ceos turned to curbing mourning itself. Besides the prescription—a recurrent one, as we saw—to carry the dead in silence, and instructions for how to accomplish particular rituals (preliminary sacrifice,

---

[33] See P. Loraux, "La théorie est trop belle: Script d'un scénario sur la 'politique' d'Aristote," *Revue des sciences humaines* 213 (1989): 9–37.

[34] For example, Plato *Laws* 12.960a (*thrēneín* and crying outside of the house, transportation of the properly covered dead, prohibition against crying during the procession) and the funeral regulation of the Labyadai (Delphi, around 400 B.C.; see F. Sokolowsky, *Lois sacrées des cités grecques* [Paris, 1969], 77c), in which we should especially note, after purely sumptuary prescriptions, the directions concerning the *ekphorá* (carrying the dead silently, properly covered; prohibition against crying outside the house and prior to arrival at the *sêma*) and the prohibitions against wailing at the cemetery over the ones already long dead and against lamenting on specific anniversary dates.

[35] As a matter of fact, the *ekphorá* is at the heart of all funeral ceremonies. Many texts, from Aeschylus's *Choephoroi* (430; also see 8) to Diodorus (11.38), testify to this by referring to the entire ceremony with this word.

[36] For Solon, see Plutarch *Solon*, 21.5–7. For Ceos, see Sokolowski, *Lois sacrées*, 97 (fifth century B.C.). For Gambreion, see Sokolowski, 16 (third century B.C.).

purifications on the following day), we should note that women going to the ceremony had to leave the *sêma* (grave) before the men (otherwise, certainly, their unbridled emotionalism would have disturbed the men and allowed lament to have the last word);[37] that only the women who had been polluted by the presence of the corpse, that is, only the closest relatives, could go to the house of the dead for the departure of the procession; that, among these polluted ones (*tàs miainoménas*), the mother held the highest rank, before wife, sisters, and daughters, and in no instance could more than five other women be added to the latter. But in the third century B.C., the "law for the people of Gambreion" begins with mention of the "mourning ones" (feminine: *tàs penthoúsas*), and the text continues by associating and distinguishing the lots of women and men. This deserves particular attention.

Just as if the mourners (the very same women who are called "the polluted ones" at Ceos) set the standard for the highest degree of mourning, the first prescription concerns their clothing. It should be gray (or brown, depending on how we picture *phaián,* which the *Suda* describes as a mixture of black and white),[38] in any case neither black nor white, but something in between. In short, a mixture, a combination of mourning colors, as if the colors themselves were a mark of excess for women—the proof being that men, as well as children, can choose: if they do not want (*eàn mề boúlōntai*) gray, they can wear white (hence we can deduce that the color carries no connotation of excess when worn by men). In addition, women's dress—and only women's—must not be "soiled"; thus gestures with which mourners soil their dress are forbidden. The excess to be prevented is by definition feminine, and taking this intrinsic weakness into account, the law allots women's mourning one month more than men's.[39]

---

[37] I do not accept the suggestion that the text be corrected by the addition of a *mề,* which hardly adds meaning to a clause now made negative.

[38] The funeral regulation of the Labyadai mentions *phaõtàn khlaînan* (Sokolowski, *Lois sacrées,* 77c6).

[39] Rites must be completed in three months; the *ándres* then end their mourning, and women come out of mourning (*exanístasthai ek tễs kēdeías*). We will recall that in

Then the magistrate assigned to women intervenes, the *gunai-konómos* elected by the people. During the sacrifices that precede the Thesmophoria, he prays to the gods for the happiness and prosperity of compliant men and obedient women (*toîs emménousin kaì taîs peithoménais tôide tôi nómōi*) and curses men who disobey and women who do not comply. Here again, we find in the words' variation the same concern to distinguish between the sexes, but there is also something new: the magistrate assigned to women ensures the link with the gods for men as well as for women, and his intervention takes places at the time of the Thesmophoria, this "political" festival of lawful wives. In addition, two steles inscribed with the law are erected, one in front of the Thesmophorion, the other in front of the temple of Artemis goddess of childbirth (*Lokhía*). Our initial impression is thus confirmed: overseeing mourning means looking after women. Hence the *gunaikonómos*—even if, at Gambreion, as in the "Solonian" legislation, this official is also in charge of punishing offenders of the opposite sex. Let us reread Plutarch regarding Solon:

> Most of these practices still survive in our laws. It has been added (*proskeîtai*)[40] that lawbreakers will be punished by the *gunaikonómos*, because they are overcome by unmanly and effeminate passions and sins in their mourning (*hōs anándrois kaì gunaikṓdesi toîs perì tà pénthē páthesi kaì hamartḗmasin enekhoménous*).
>
> (Plutarch *Solon* 21.5)

(Is being a mourner in the masculine synonymous with being "effeminate"? Let us beware. For a long time, men will eschew all passion in mourning. Thus Laertes in *Hamlet* will not shed one tear

---

other contexts, *exanístasthai* can be translated as "resuscitate." Women must recover from mourning as they recover from childbirth, but men are content to break it off (*lúein tà pénthē*). Throughout the text, great care is taken to distinguish women's from men's lot, and even if we take into account the desire for "variation," the choice of wording is meaningful.

[40] For Jacoby, this word is formal proof of the late introduction of *gunaikonómoi* in the context of legislation aimed at moral restoration.

on Ophelia's grave, he who, upon hearing of his sister's death, for an instant let himself be overcome by women's cries:

> Too much of water hast thou, poor Ophelia,
> And therefore I forbid my tears; but yet
> It is our trick; nature her custom holds,
> Let shame say what it will: when these are gone,
> The woman will be out.
>
> (*Hamlet* 4.7.184–88)

Or witness Archilochus, less anachronistically, who, to incite his friends to "drive effeminate mourning away," mimics in his poem the rejection of the feminine by replacing *odúnē,* the inner suffering so well known by women, with a manly wound that keeps on bleeding but can be healed.)[41]

If mourning is feminine as such, it is also an opportunity to repress femininity among males: thus the *gunaikonómos* does not really step outside his function,[42] which is, according to the narrowest definition, to regulate women's behavior, to punish those who do not submit to authority, and, "along with the Areopagites, to watch over gatherings (*súnodoi*) that take place in homes (*oikíai*) during weddings and sacrifices."[43] Gatherings inside the *oikía* are dangerous because a wife could face temptation there. What, then, can we say about the *éxodoi,* those "outings"—codified or not—of women, outside their houses, which cities attempt to control very strictly?[44]

---

[41] Archilochus frag. 13 West, lines 4–5 and 8, with commentary by A. Pippin Burnett, *Three Archaic Poets* (Cambridge, 1983), 47–48; on feminine *odúnē* and the manly wound, see Loraux, *Experiences of Tiresias,* 31–37 and 88–100.

[42] A very Greek function, and one that Rome does not recognize: even the *aediles* have no such duty in their jurisdiction. We should distinguish carefully between the *astunómoi,* who can impose a tax on prostitutes, and the *gunaikonómoi,* who are concerned only with female "citizens," although they punish women *katà toùs hodoús akosmoúsas* (*Suda* s.v.).

[43] See Pollux 8.112 for the *kósmos* of women, Philochorus frag. 65 for the quotation, and Menander the Rhetor *Perì epikēdeíōn* 3.364.1 (Spengel) on this function, which is assigned to one elected by show of hands and is widespread in cities.

[44] On *éxodoi,* see the law of Gambreion, lines 15–16, where Sokolowski under-

For even when it is a matter of accompanying one's "own" dead, it is better for a woman not to go out into the streets (*katà toùs hodoús*). This is, doubtless, an opportunity also to understand in retrospect the shared reluctance to admit women to the *ekphorá*, the funeral procession that passes through the city and is at the heart of the funeral ceremony, as opposed to the *próthesis*, enclosed within the house, where women hold their natural place.[45]

Ideally, feminine sorrow should be hermetically sealed inside the house, especially when the mourning woman is a bereaved mother who weeps over her son. This is how the messenger interprets Eurydice's silent flight after she learns of Haemon's death in the *Antigone*:

> I am sustained with hope
> that after she hears the sorrow of her son,
> she will not ask for a lament
> throughout the city but will order (*prothésein*)[46]
> her servants to moan her own mourning (*pénthos oikeîon sténein*)
> inside the house (*hupò stégēs ésō*).
> For she is not so inexperienced in judgment
> that she would commit a mistake (*hamartánein*).
>
> (Sophocles *Antigone* 1246–50)

The mistake—the audience soon learns—is a tragic one: just as the chorus feared, Eurydice commits suicide. But for the moment, the messenger's answer can be understood in its more obvious sense, as an observation on legal transgressions (*hamártēma*, said Plutarch with reference to Solonian legislation) or on the unseemliness, for the queen's feminine honor, inherent in lamenting throughout the city. As for the *pénthos oikeîon*, for Eurydice it is Haemon's death, which she already

---

stands these "outings" as prescribed for the period of mourning. Also see Plato *Laws* 6.784d on restrictions on "outings" for women who do not obey marital imperatives; see also Plutarch *Solon* 21.5.

[45] It is interesting to note that it is while she is following the procession (*ekphorá*) of her mother-in-law that the wife of the Athenian Euphiletos is seen by Eratosthenes, who then seeks her out and becomes her lover (Lysias *On the Murder of Eratosthenes* 8).

[46] How can we not be reminded of the *próthesis* suggested in *prothésein*?

has anticipated when she comes on stage to inquire about "the rumor of a calamity concerning her kin" (1187: *oikeíou kakoû*). P. Mazon translates *pénthos oikeîon* as "intimate mourning" ("deuil intime"), and before I settled on "her own mourning" ("*son* deuil"), I hesitated between "familial mourning" ("deuil familial") and "mourning (so) close or nearby" ("deuil [si] proche"). Applied to the relationship between a mother and her son, *oikeîon* has all the connotations that make it a marker for what is familial, close, and thus by virtue of the tragic dialectic of the *génos* and of the self, for what is "one's *own*."[47] What loss is more "one's own" for a mother than the loss of one who is closest to her? But in *oikeîon* we should also understand, in line with its etymology, what takes place inside the house. This is the masculine solution, or at any rate, the civic way of assigning limits to the loss of self, limits that for women are the familiar walls of the *oîkos*. The reasoning is that the *oikeîon pénthos* must not contaminate the city, just as, more generally, funeral rites should not intrude on the political institutions' operations. When this happens in spite of everything, it is a sure sign of problems in the city. We are reminded of Theramenes, who took the opportunity when parents (*suggeneîs*) gathered for the festival of the Apaturia, to organize a procession of mourning men, who walked toward the assembly as if they were the parents (*suggeneîs*) of those dead in the battle of Arginusae.[48] The spectacle of mourning men should be seen only in funeral processions; because this gloomy procession was going in the direction of the assembly, the expected outcome is the condemnation to death of the *stratēgoí,* and this is what actually happens.

The city thus protects itself against funeral ceremonies, in which some cities even forbid their officials to participate,[49] and against women, their emotionalism, and their excesses. By using this word, I do not mean to evoke, as some may think, the existence—even

[47] On the spectrum of connotations of *oikeîon,* see N. Loraux, "La guerra nella famiglia," *Studi storici* 28 (1987): 5–35, and "La main d'Antigone," *Mètis* 1 (1986): 165–96.

[48] Xenophon *Hellenica* 1.7.8.

[49] See the law of Tegea (fourth century B.C.) in Sokolowski, *Supplément,* 31.7.

potential—of some "political" demonstration by women, born out of mourning. However strong our desire to confirm the effectiveness of so many civic precautions, or, conversely, to make sure that there actually were tense moments when female excess threatened political order, we are compelled to renounce it. It is extremely unlikely that, coming back from the cemetery, Greek women ever marched into their city's agora to make demands, or, like the mothers of the Plaza de Mayo, to ask for justice. I base this last remark less on the absence of any historical evidence (it is always possible to imagine that there is censorship in historiographical prose of everything that concerns women) than on the structural impossibility of such a hypothesis. There is no need to appeal to the all too well-known and so often commented-upon "political exclusion" of Greek women. Considering only the very specific status of mourning women in funerals, considering the small number to which female relatives are usually reduced, how could we imagine any female insubordination other than a fit of despair badly held in check by the ritual?

Certainly, abandoning the realm of facts to question the constructions of fiction, we will encounter in Athenian tragedy Euripides' mourning band of suppliants, seeking decent funeral for the seven leaders who fell before Thebes. And, if we agree to accept a case of solitary rebellion, how could we not think of Antigone, who resists Creon simply by performing the funeral rites forbidden by the tyrant?

But fiction itself stops at the limits of the thinkable: what the Seven's mothers or Polynices' sister is demanding is nothing more than the normal performance of standard funeral rites. As long as funeral rites are performed according to the rules, there is no feminine drift toward the unknown. In addition, it is a man—a fallen king, Adrastus—who leads the mourning mothers to Theseus in the *Suppliant Women,* and Antigone is after all a solitary conspirator—in other words, an oxymoron. To proceed, as many do, to equate Oedipus's daughter with a rebel, I would have to forget so many Greek particulars! I would have to forget that Antigone wants to honor Polynices' dead body, and not to "overthrow" Creon or politically rehabilitate her brother's reputation. I would also have to forget that Antigone would not have gone against the regent's orders if the dead man were her husband instead of her brother . . .[50] Finally and especially, I would have to forget that Antigone is a tragic character, and, as such, she bears witness to the limits beyond which the thinkable cannot be subverted.

Let us set aside the overly realist hypothesis of a funeral that degenerates into a "political" demonstration of mothers. Rather let us record what tragic freedom consists of and what constraints are called for to make a fiction acceptable. What does the city fear in female mourning?

Without anticipating the rest of this study too much, I will suggest that this fear belongs to an entirely different order than a fear of any impending action. This different order is that of the representations that *ándres* make of the woman-mother. But patience is required! We are still focused on the subject of funeral legislation, in which mothers are included in the group of close relatives. Before long, tragedy hands them back their status of exemplary mourners, and the suppliants beg Theseus to "take the mother's side."[51] Civic laws mean to curb maternal mourning; tragedy, because it distinguishes between the political and the nonpolitical sphere, recognizes that mothers alone are in fact the true regulators of mourning, before checking again, in a very civic way, the predictable excess of their grief—mothers will not see their sons dead.

But we have not yet come to tragedy. We are still not done with our examination of the practices whose aim is to channel feminine excess.

---

[50] I will come back to this topic soon, in *La famille d'Oedipe,* to be published in La Librairie du XXe Siècle.

[51] Euripides *Suppliant Women* 377.

The Effective Tears of Matrons

As we study these mourning practices, we will perhaps conclude that this is Greek behavior, normal in a Mediterranean land. And to back up such an observation, we might cite the work of E. De Martino, who has written a book on lamentation "in the ancient world," using the *pianto* from Sardinia, Corsica, and Luca to illuminate the *thrênos*. But as far as historical reflection goes, we should not be content with the deus ex machina of continuity if we want to avoid the dreaded objection of "evidence," an objection that continually confronts anyone who, while interested in the most widespread social practices, focuses on their specificity. What is more like a funeral lament than a funeral lament? Such is the urgent question posed by factual history, stubborn in its clear conscience. The "ancient Mediterranean stock" is no help then; we must distance ourselves and play the game of "comparatism." Thus, when viewed from the vantage point of Rome, the extent of the civic precautions of the *ándres* appears even more remarkable.

Not that in Rome women are not supposed to mourn their children; the topos of a feminine nature prone to tears is just as prevalent there. The historians tell how Fabius Maximus had to silence women's laments by confining matrons to their homes, *intra suum quamque limen,* after the defeat at Cannae.[1]

Let us return to the story of Coriolanus, which is punctuated with women's tears at every stage, and particularly in Dionysius of Halicarnassus's account, which is loquacious yet very enlightening about the difference between Greek practice and Roman management of female mourning. It is precisely women's tears that make Coriolanus fall into the trap of his own ill-controlled affectivity: such is Valeria's plan in Plutarch, a plan that, as we know, is successful in all respects. Livy, moreover, credits all the Roman matrons for this plan, giving the entire episode another, much more political, dimension.[2]

The word *matrona,* first and foremost a legal term, the denomination of a woman by reference to her status as married woman,[3] seems to imply something like a quasi-official intervention by the *civitas* as an appointed body. In fact, even if the canonical Roman interpretation of this episode only mentions "women" and women's tears, and even if, despite the presence of two matrons as leaders—the mother and the wife[4]—the group that supplicates the public enemy is referred to only as *ingens mulierum agmen,* and, finally, even if it is to the *Fortuna* of women[5] that Rome raises a temple in thanks for its safety, the enterprise has, for a Roman historian of Rome, a collective subject

---

[1] Plutarch *Fabius Maximus* 17.7; Livy 22.55.6. During civil conflicts, it even happens that women are forbidden to mourn (including Gaius Gracchus's wife, according to Plutarch *Gaius Gracchus* 17.6) or that mothers' tears are likened to a crime of conspiracy against the empire and are punishable with death (Tacitus *Annals* 6.10).

[2] Livy 2.1–2.

[3] A matron is a woman fated to give birth in wedlock, and she keeps the name whether she actually becomes a mother, a widow, or remains childless. See Thomas, "Le ventre, corps maternel, droit paternel," p. 221 and n.71; also E. Benveniste, *Vocabulaire des institutions indo-européennes* (Paris, 1969), 1:243, on *matrimonium* as the "legal condition of a *mater.*" The Greek translation of *matrona* is, in Dionysius of Halicarnassus, *gunaîkes gametaí* (married women, 8.56), and it is significant that this title is given by a divine voice, during a ceremony in which statues are consecrated.

[4] This wife is herself a matron; Livy uses the juridical terms *mater, coniunx,* and *liberi* at 2.40.4.

[5] Plutarch *Coriolanus* 37.3–4: *Túkhē gunaikeía;* Dionysius of Halicarnassus 8.55: *Túkhē gunaikôn;* Livy 2.40.11–12.

whose designation is a matter of a very different order than the difference between the sexes alone. Further, even if the *civitas* recognizes a
civic function of tears, it is because there is the same gap between
feminine tears and matrons' tears as that dividing a topos from a
political act—and the very thing that could not even be sought in
Greece is found in Rome.

To put it differently, Roman women are split, as it were, between
"the habitual tumult of feminine suffering" and the put-on tearless
mourning of the matron. Pain in the shape of a wound makes her the
equal of a soldier covered with scars.[6] But if there are two ways for a
mother to mourn a son, only one of them—Livia's as she mourns
Drusus; Cornelia's, mother of the Gracchi; or Attia's—is peculiarly
Roman, insofar as it characterizes the matron as much more than a
woman.[7]

Now the Roman city (and herein lies its originality) knows how to
make a distinction in the case of women between manly heroism and
femininity. Funeral legislation assigns tears to ordinary women, each
one immersed in her woman's life. Since "women cry by nature," the
city recorded that fact and assigned time limits (nine months for
widows, ten for mourning a father, a son, or a brother),[8] "to compro-

---

[6] Seneca *Consolation to Helvia* 3.1. His scars of the soul, however, hold no glory,
unlike those that are inscribed on the soldier's body and that are a symbol of his valor
(cf. Plutarch *Coriolanus* 14.2, 15.1).

[7] On Livia and Cornelia, see Seneca *Consolation to Marcia* 2–3 and 16 (for more
about Cornelia, see *Helvia* 16 and Plutarch *Gaius Gracchus* 19.3); on Attia, see Pliny
Letters 3.16. Octavia represents the opposite model (Seneca *Marcia* 2). On those
women "whose conspicuous bravery put them in the rank of great men" see Seneca
Helvia 16.

[8] Nine or ten months for a widow: Seneca *Helvia* 16.1; Plutarch *Numa* 12.3; in
the Twelve Tables, the duration of widowhood is modeled on that of pregnancy. Ten
months also represents, before Caesar's time, the duration of a civil year, which is the
time allotted to the mourning of a father, a son, or a brother (Plutarch *Coriolanus*
39.10). As a matter of fact, it is the longest term of mourning, as fixed by Numa
(Plutarch *Numa* 12.3). By way of comparison, we might recall that mourning lasts
twelve days in Sparta, one month in Athens and Argos; in Gambreion, even though
women are allowed one month more than men, mourning's duration does not
exceed four months Here again we can detect Greek reticence toward mourning.

mise with the stubbornness of female sorrow by way of a public decree (*publica constitutione*)."[9]

Roman norms of mourning are imperatives, then—and the matrons seem to have set themselves up as guardians of their strict observance[10]—but they also adjust to reality when exceptional circumstances or the severity of a defeat throws the entire civic body into distress. After Cannae, Fabius Maximus assigns a place and a time to *pénthos* (at home and up to thirty days if desired), while prescribing that the city must be purified from all mourning when the period is past.[11]

To come back to the initiative of women in the story of Coriolanus, we can now add that after Coriolanus died as a result of the Volscians' anger, according to Plutarch (and Dionysius of Halicarnassus, although Livy relates no such event),[12] the people accepted the women's demand to extend collective mourning to ten months, "as it was customary for each one to do for a father, a son, or a brother." They were like so many mothers to Coriolanus; thus they perform again in this particular case the same gesture they once did, according to tradition, for Brutus and Publicola. On the interpretation of such a gesture, however, Roman historiographers differ from Greek historians of Rome: the latter emphasize the opposition between public and private (*dēmosíai / idíai*), between the official decision of the *dêmos* and the private counsel of women among themselves, one by one and group by group;[13] the former particularly insist

---

[9] Seneca *Helvia* 16.1.

[10] In fragment 73 (F. Haase) of Seneca's *De matrimonio*, Marcia, Cato's youngest daughter, when asked about the limit of her mourning, answers: "That of my life." The matrons are keeping watch . . .

[11] Plutarch *Fabius Maximus* 18.1

[12] Plutarch (*Coriolanus* 39.10) and Dionysius of Halicarnassus (8.62.2) describe the mourning of the Romans and their wives; Livy does not mention mourning at all.

[13] Plutarch *Publicola* 23.4 (the people vote on public funerals, *dēmosíai*, and everyone contributes a quarter of an *as*, but women come to an agreement between themselves, *idíai*); Dionysius of Halicarnassus 8.62.2 (for Coriolanus, the mourning

on the actual political meaning of the act. Thus for Brutus, the avenger of a matron, women assume their part of public sorrow (*publica maestitia*) by mourning him for a year, just as they would do for a father (*ut parentem*)—but beneath this reference to the private sphere, does not Livy actually slip in an allusion to the notion of *parens patriae* 'father of the country'? The same is true of Publicola, so poor that he did not leave enough to pay for his own funeral, which the state takes upon itself, and whom the matrons mourn as they mourned Brutus.[14] We must also take into account the long duration of such practices, since their meaning remained stable from the first years of the Republic to the beginnings of the imperial era. This is attested by a decree of Piso in A.D. 2, decided by all the *decuriones* and the *coloni,* that regulates funeral honors for Gaius Caesar, adoptive son of Augustus, and that specifies that the *matronae*—again—will mourn him, joining in the public grief.[15] Doubtless, their "initiative" has degenerated into obedience to a decision, but the essential fact remains that Roman women, under the title of matron, have a share in public mourning from the time of the newly born Republic up to Augustus's reign.

From Greek cities to Rome, we cannot emphasize enough that they differ in all respects in their behavior toward mothers in mourning: mourning is strictly contained in the sphere of close family ties for Greek women, and thus subjected to many restrictions, while women's mourning in Rome is limited but recognized in its private sense, and always liable to become a public display by part of the city. Seeing such a gap between two civic ways of assigning a place to the feminine element in the management of mourning, we could certainly try to understand it as an echo, as it were, of the deep differ-

---

of the Romans is *idíāi kaì dēmosíāi,* but women, as is their custom [*nómos*] in private mourning, mourn him for a year).

[14] On Brutus, see Livy 2.7.4; on Publicola, 2.16.7 (*de publico est datus. Luxere matronae ut Brutum*).

[15] Dessau, *Inscriptiones Latinae Selectae,* 140 (funeral honors dedicated to C. Caesar).

ence—from the *póleis* to the *civitas*—between Greek and Roman enunciation of the familial and the public.[16] On the Greek side, we will emphasize the contentious relation between the *oîkos* and the city, while in Rome the family is the essential basis of civic life. We need only compare "public funerals" in Rome with the similarly named ceremony in Athens:[17] here, the dead are cut off from all familial bonds and taken over by the collective group; there, the deceased belong to great families, who seize the opportunity of the ceremony to offer themselves as examples to the entire city. In Rome, the *gens* is exalted through the praise of one of its members, a great man, but also a great woman; in Athens, abstract *ándres* are eulogized collectively in front of a male public, with only a few female kinfolk interspersed.[18]

We can, I think, here bring to an end a comparison that has been shown to be well founded. Leaving Rome behind (not without regret, for the pleasure of the difference is great), let us pursue the investigation in Greek territory, since such mistrust of feminine and maternal grief is evidently distinctive of Greek cities.

---

[16] This difference between *pólis,* an entity all-powerful over the units that constitute it, and *civitas,* a vast "mutuality" of reciprocal relations, is already apparent in language. See E. Benveniste, "Deux modèles linguistiques de la cité," in *Problèmes de linguistique générale* (Paris, 1974), 2:272–80.

[17] See Loraux, *Invention of Athens,* 43.

[18] Keeping in mind that in Sparta the mourning of kings is a matter for women as well as for men, we might wonder whether we should see the mark of an aristocratic society in the position accorded to women from Sparta to Rome.

The *Páthos* of a Mother

To illuminate the city's mistrust of feminine grief, we need to approach things from the other end, and to focus on the most intimate of griefs, that of the mother in mourning, who is so isolated in her singularity. So true is it that silence surrounds nameless Greek women that our only recourse from this point on is to cling to the texts, poetic or tragic, which alone give an illustrious name and a central place to the figure of the mourning mother. There the intimacy of grief is a result of an intensification of the feeling of corporeal closeness, made all the more acute because it is never felt as much as it is after a loss.

We cannot arrive at the intimate without taking many detours. First, unavoidably, we encounter the codified gestures of ritual, gestures that are the same for all women, and that, by stylizing the twinges of her despair, allow each mother to express her own mourning with the generic signs of mourning.

Thus, from epic on, the mother is the one whose grief, suddenly expressed, gives the signal of social mourning.[1] She is the one who closes the eyelids of a dead son—and the dying Polynices asks this very

[1] She is the one who starts the crisis that constitutes, according to De Martino (*Morte e pianto rituale*, 195 f.), the first stage of lament.

35

gesture from Jocasta in his prayer in the *Phoenician Women*.[2] The mother is the one above all who first utters the heart-rending lament, before there are funerals where mourning becomes domesticated into a ceremony. Thus Hecuba, who from the heights of Troy's walls sees Achilles kill Hector and who takes off her veil, tears her hair, and emits a piercing shout (*kṓkusen*); after her, the father moans (*ṓimōxen*), and the people echo shouts and laments; but it is especially meaningful that in the same line the head of the dead hero is covered with dust, and the mother stands up in despair.[3] Since his own mother has already been taken away and enslaved, it is Hecuba again who will lament over the dead child Astyanax: she is his father's mother, but for the child she has no other name than *mḗtēr*, and it is this title that the chorus intuitively gives her—"Lament, Mother!"[4] And it is Jocasta again who utters the *thrḗnos* over her dying sons.[5] Here we are immersed in epic, and in Euripidean tragedy, where a rereading of Homer is evident, with the exception that the Iliadic Hecuba knows the difference between spontaneous lament and the *thrḗnos* in verse, which is sung only during the ceremony, later then—but it is true that if Plutarch is to be believed, even Solon did not make a distinction between pure wailing and versified lament.

Long before the ritual, there is the mother's crying, which accompanies the vision of the corpse that used to be a son; during the delay imposed by the ritual care of the corpse, there is the body of the mother clinging to that of the dead son. To hold in their arms what is "bloody, yet still the treasure of a mother," such is the wish of Euripides' suppliant mothers, who know, asking for their sons' remains,

---

[2] Euripides *Phoenician Women* 1451–52; see E. Vermeule, *Aspects of Death in Early Greek Art and Poetry* (Berkeley, 1979), 14–15.

[3] *Iliad* 22.405–7.

[4] Euripides *Trojan Women* 1229; see also lines 1145–46, 1181, and 1212.

[5] Euripides *Phoenician Women* 1433–35. Moreover, it is not certain that we must give a specific translation of the verb *ethrḗnei*, because, as G. Nagy observes in *The Best of the Achaeans* (Baltimore, 1979), 112 and note, tragedy usually does not preserve the semantic distinction between *góoi* (the lament sung by relatives) and *thrḗnoi* (sung by professional poets).

that they will obtain both an end to their suffering and an increase of their pain.[6] As a good civic leader, Theseus will make sure that they do not *see* those bodies disfigured by blood: just as in official funerals in Athens, they will have a right only to the bones of the funeral pyre, pure abstraction of the beloved body.

The sight of a son's corpse is *páthos* in the highest degree: for Jocasta, whom the sight of the calamity fills with excessive suffering (*huperpathḗsasa*); for Hecuba, who, in the *Iliad,* regains speech only to question a life that is accompanied by the horrible suffering (*ainà pathoûsa*) caused by Hector's death.[7] Suddenly present with a heart-rending accuracy, the grief and the memory of the intimacy of these bodies produce excessive pain for the body-memory of mothers. Euripidean tragedy has much to say about this sensual intensity that expresses itself only on a background of loss. Thus, for example, Andromache's good-bye to the child Astyanax who is about to die:

> O young nursling dearest to your mother,
> O sweet breath of your skin, . . .
>
> . . . .
>
> now, never again, kiss your mother,
> throw yourself at her who bore you, and entwine your arms
> around me and kiss me.[8]
>
> (Euripides *Trojan Women* 757–63)

And then there is what Hecuba tells Hector to divert him from waiting for Achilles and death. Priam has spoken at length and moaned over his own fate, he whom Hector's death will leave to

---

[6] Euripides *Suppliant Women* 368–71; besides the oxymoron constituted by *matéros ágalma phónion,* we should note that *ágalma* is both treasure and statue. How far are we from the problematic of the double? On Theseus and the ban on seeing, see lines 941–49.

[7] Euripides *Phoenician Women* 1455–56; *Iliad* 22.433–35.

[8] We might compare this with the welcome that Jocasta in the *Phoenician Women* (304–16) gives Polynices, who is threatened with death

disaster. Hecuba laments and weeps, uncovers her breast,[9] and reminds her son who is about to die of the time when she gave him the shelter of the breast "where one forgets one's cares"; it is to the child that she once offered her breast, but the adjective *lathikēdḗs* can apply only to the man—the anxious man, who is compelled to heroism and knows it, and will not listen, even if she insists (*tôn mnêsai* 'Remember it [your mother's body]'). And she adds, bringing us back to mourning ritual:

> If he kills you, I shall *no longer*[10] be able to weep
> over your bier, dear child, whom I myself begat.
>
> (*Iliad* 22.86–87)

As if mourning necessarily were part of a mother's fate from the very beginning, Hecuba has so much anticipated the vision, both dreaded and strangely comforting, of Hector's *próthesis* that the mother panics in front of her son destined to die at a ferocious adversary's hands, foreseeing the loss of her son and of his dead body, as well as of the comfort brought on by ritual. Hecuba thus evokes the past of the blissful proximity of bodies for Hector, a man without a present, and the future of the ritual that has been imagined so often and will not actually take place. And here, without further mediation, the gestures of funerals appear to graft themselves on the very ancient intimacy that has been forever lost, the intimacy between mother and small child. This is a way of suggesting that a mother owes her preeminent position alongside the dead to the unconditional privilege given once and for all by the bond of childbirth. A bond that is without mediation, exacting, painful, and that Euripides' choruses sometimes describe as "terrible": terribly tender, terribly strong, simply *terrible*.[11] That very thing that makes of the "race of women" a

---

[9] On this gesture, see N. Loraux, "*Matrem nudam:* Quelques versions grecques," *L'écrit du temps* 11 (1986): 90–102.

[10] Translators often forget this word, which suggests that Hecuba is doomed to lament Hector eternally.

[11] *Phoenician Women* 355–56; *Iphigenia at Aulis* 917–18.

philóteknon génos (a "race" that loves its children), by welding forevermore the maternal body to the memory of the newborn: what Greek men would like to take away from women so badly.[12]

Thus Homeric mothers, not only Hecuba, but also Demeter, recall they are the birthgivers. And, in order to designate the child as what is both the most precious and the most heartrending possession of a mother, Euripidean tragedy readily calls it the *lókheuma,* the product of childbirth.[13] Bolder yet and to accuse Agamemnon of Iphigenia's murder with greater effect, Clytemnestra, in Aeschylus, claims that her hated husband has sacrificed "his child, my dear pain" (*philtátēn emoi ōdîna*).[14] *Odís* describes the searing pangs of childbirth; designated as *ōdís* beyond death, the young daughter Iphigenia incarnates for her mother a life that has barely been detached from her own body and whose loss her mother feels all the more in an instant of sinister repetition of the wrenching of the ultimate separation—as if Clytemnestra could not stop giving birth in endless parturition as long as her daughter lived. Certainly it is a matter for Roman jurists to record "the opacity of the maternal body to the law."[15] But there is something like an intuition of this opaque otherness in Greek tragedy, and the Clytemnestra of the *Oresteia* is its mighty symbol.

Of course, there always exists a Praxithea to postulate another hierarchy, where autochthony is worth more than reproduction, and where childbirth rights yield before those of the city. Praxithea then bows and exults in her very renunciation. But if the queen of Athens

[12] See Loraux, *Experiences of Tiresias,* 12–16.

[13] *Homeric Hymn to Demeter* 66. For *lókheuma,* see Euripides *Phoenician Women* 803, 815–16, and *Erechtheus,* frag. 10 Carrara, line 50.

[14] *Agamemnon* 1417–18. See J. Dumortier, *Le vocabulaire médical d'Eschyle et les écrits hippocratiques,* 2d ed. (Paris, 1975), 27–28, on *Iphigenia in Tauris* 1102 (where Artemis is Leto's *ōdís*). We should note that *ōdís* is not only, as Dumortier would have it, the child in relation to a woman, but the *daughter* in relation to her mother.

[15] "L'opacité du corps maternel au droit": Thomas, "Le ventre, corps maternel, droit paternel," 225; on the decisive importance of the corporeal separation of the child (in this case, of course, a son) from the mother in Roman law, see also Thomas, p. 222.

looks like the heroine of autochthony, at least she is not a tragic queen. Because there is in tragedy a scale of values—scandalous, certainly, in the sight of civic orthodoxy, and that would be threatening outside of theatrical representation—for mothers as such, by virtue of which the child is the first, indeed the only, treasure and is of absolutely prime importance for the city.

Once again, let us return to Hecuba, paradigm of mourning motherhood. About Polyxena, whom Odysseus leads to sacrifice, she claims:

> Through her I rejoice, and I forget my misfortunes (*epiléthomai kakôn*);[16]
> she is a comfort to me for many things,
> city, nurse, staff, leader on the road.[17]
>
> (Euripides *Hecuba* 279–81)

Polyxena is my city: an utterance that would be impossible and virtually forbidden to women in Athens outside of the theater—women, who do not have the title of "citizen" but must devote themselves to the city. Hecuba, it is true, is queen and barbarian, and, like a good Greek, Odysseus throws back at her the image of the genuine city, where the man of valor—in this case Achilles—is more honored than the coward. The word of a man against the word of a mother: if Hecuba were not so already, she is defeated now, and in the future she will be called *ápais ápolis*, childless, cityless. The same is true again in the *Trojan Women:* Andromache has already gone to the ship of her master while Astyanax is led to his death. Hecuba, then, remains in the role of the mother, whose laments create what seems to be an equivalence between the city and the child (to Astyanax, she

---

[16] For the Iliadic Hecuba, in relation to whom the text of Euripides places itself, it was the breast that gave the child forgetfulness of his cares. The exchange is total.

[17] At *Iliad* 22.432–34, Hecuba says of Hector that he was night and day her pride throughout the city (*katà ástu*). This is a big step forward. *Ápais, ápolis*: Hecuba 669 and 810–11.

says: "Alas for the city! Alas for you!"). Once more, Hecuba is the old woman, *ápolis, áteknos.*[18]

Immediately confirmed over the body of the child, the incommensurable character of the loss establishes itself as patently obvious. Grief then becomes wrath and, sometimes, action.

[18] Eurıpıdes *Trojan Women* 795–96, 1186.

Black Wrath

It falls to goddesses—to those among them who are mothers—to go farther, in the myth and the ritual that give them credit for having taken the step toward action: from sorrow to wrath,[1] from wrath to secession. As for the mythical queens of tragedy, who are deprived of the weapon of secession, they will go as far as murder, as we shall see.[2]

From sorrow to wrath: while we are still questioning whether it could even be contemplated, the step has already been taken in the texts. The question is a persistent one to judge by the insistent doubt surrounding the very possibility of such a sequence. I do not know whether we should ascribe this to our perfectly sterile mourning practices, to our occidental inability to decenter ourselves (although contemporary examples of such a contiguity between loss and the explosion of wrath are certainly not lacking), or to a very powerful desire for forgetfulness—this forgetting of origins we still call civilization . . . It is of great importance to illuminate this point, if only to

---

[1] Contra P. Lévêque, who, eager to rediscover the theme of the Goddess's *primordial* wrath, dissociates very strongly wrath and mourning ("Structures imaginaires et fonctionnement des mystères grecs," *Studi storico-religiosi* 6 [1982]: 185–208, especially pp. 190–93), I think that the transition from mourning to wrath is essential to the figure of a divine Mother.

[2] I would readily apply to tragedy M. Alexiou's observation that mourning is always more exacerbated where the law of vendetta flourishes (*Ritual Lament,* 22).

understand better why we are so eager to establish that the Greeks ultimately are removed, distant, from us. But such an inquiry would take us much farther, and for the time being I will confine myself to a few Greek examples, hoping that their apparent strangeness can still awaken some echo in the present of our affects.

From sorrow to wrath, then. Thus Achilles, mourning Patroclus's death, is compared to a lion—a lioness?—whose young have been snatched by a hunter and who despairs: a "bitter wrath" fills him, and this wrath announces the hopeless wrath lying in the depths of the hero's sobs. We should also evoke the shift in Eurydice's feelings postulated by the messenger in the *Antigone,* from the *pénthos oikeîon* to the exasperated heart that conceals a secret in the dark.[3]

This brings us back to mothers, and to the notion of a sorrow that does not forget and feeds on itself, and that is dangerous for those around the mother whose mourning has congealed into a confrontation with herself and others. This sorrow transformed into defiance has the dreaded name of that memory-wrath the Greeks have called *mênis* ever since the *Iliad* and Achilles' wrath.

Mênis: black like a child of the night, it is terrible and it lasts.[4] It is repetitive and endless, all the more so since never to have an end is precisely the motivating force of *mênis.* Thus a motionless "always" (*aeí*) establishes itself, ready to vie endlessly with the political meaning of *aeí* that tells, on the contrary, of a continuity in the service of the city, a continuity that nothing must break. But I shall not expand on *mênis* again.[5] Let us rather turn to the story of Demeter.

Abducted by Hades, the young Persephone is as if dead for her

---

[3] *Iliad* 18.318–23; *Antigone* 1249 and 1254. De Martino (*Morte e pianto rituale,* 221–22) considers fury to be one of the essential modes of expression in crises.

[4] I do not adopt, for all that, the popular etymology that has linked this word to *ménō* ever since the ancients. As regards the real etymology, I am not able to choose philologically between the one proposed by C. Watkins, "A propos de *mênis*," *Bulletin de la Société de linguistique* (1977), 187–209, and that suggested by P. Considine, "The Etymology of *Mênis*," in *Studies in Honor of T. B. L. Webster* (Bristol, 1986), 1:53–64, but Watkins's reflections on *mênis*-memory are richer than the somewhat repetitive remarks of Considine. See now L. Muellner, *The Anger of Achilles, Mênis in Greek Epic* (Ithaca, 1996).

[5] See Loraux, "Amnesty and Its Opposite," and *Experiences of Tiresias,* 189–92.

mother, who, just as Hecuba hermetically shut herself off in her veils to weep over the loss of Polyxena,[6] shuts herself off in a dark *péplos* that insulates her from the world: "She was walking behind, grieving in her heart, veiled from head to foot; the dark robe covering the supple feet of the goddess. . . . She sat down and put the veil back on her face with her hand; for a long time, she sat on this seat, mute from grief" (*Hymn to Demeter* 181–83).[7] We might think of imprisonment inside a stone, indeed of metamorphosis into rock, perhaps thereby evoking the ultimate metaphor of this confinement: Niobe, who still sheds tears as a rock raised on Mount Sipylus, gives her name to this figure.[8] The Homeric Niobe has lost her twelve children, and the world becomes petrified around her for nine days. When she comes back to life for her people, Niobe eats a little—the length of one line of the *Iliad*—then goes back to her rocky state, a rock that weeps, and "cooks her sorrow" (*kḗdea péssei*): thus Achilles, during a pause after he has had his fill of sobbing, evokes this pain that breaks off only to reclaim its endless watch more intensely.[9]

We will meet Niobe again, but let us first go back to Demeter and her *ákhos* (her pain),[10] always retranscribed into fury (*khólos, mênis ainé, thumôi khoōménē*).[11] This fury isolates itself and flees all community: "angry with Cronides of the dark clouds," Demeter straightaway

---

[6] Euripides *Hecuba* 487.

[7] *Homeric Hymn to Demeter* 181–83, 195. On the "black-garbed goddess" as "a metonym of the wrathful, avenging goddess," see L. Slatkin, "The Wrath of Thetis," *Transactions of the American Philological Society* 116 (1986): 1–24, especially p. 18.

[8] Cf. Pausanias 1.21.3 and 8.2.5–7, as well as, for the metamorphosis, Ovid *Metamorphoses* 6.303–10.

[9] *Iliad* 24.601–7. Whether the petrification theme predates Homer or not, I see no reason to dispute (but cf. J. T. Kakridis, *Homeric Researches* [Lund, 1949], 96–105, especially p. 99) the coherence of a superbly contrasted development, as is often the case in Homeric epic. Niobe "thinks of eating" *and* becomes the rock that weeps forevermore. We should note that Achilles suggests the example of a mother as a model for Priam's paternal mourning, as if only a mother could really understand pain.

[10] A pain that constitutes her being, giving her the epithet *Akhaiá* in Athens. See Nagy, *Best of the Achaeans*, 84–85.

[11] See the sound remarks of C. Segal, "Orality, Repetition, and Formulaic Artistry in the *Homeric Hymn to Demeter*," in *I poemi rapsodici non omerici e la tradizione orale* (Padua, 1981), 107–60, especially pp. 145–46.

leaves the assembly of the gods (*nosphistheîsa theôn agorên*),[12] this place of divine sociability, to go to the world of men, their towns (or, even better, their cities), and their labors. As soon as she arrives among men, here again the goddess deliberately stands apart:

> Grieving in her heart, she sat near the road, by the well of the Virgins, where people from the city came to draw water. She was in the shade—above her grew an olive thicket—and looked like a very old woman, deprived of the gifts of childbirth and Aphrodite who loves garlands: such are the nurses of the kings who give justice.
>
> (*Homeric Hymn to Demeter* 98–104)

Coming to a stop at the Virgins' well—precisely where the virgins, the daughters of the king of Eleusis, will come—looking like an old nurse, Demeter has erased all traces of her motherhood,[13] as if better to show that she has been stripped of it. Moreover, in her mourning, she delights in emphasizing her isolation.[14] Whence the ingenuous question of the young girls ("Why did you move away from the city [*nósphi pólēos*], instead of coming near to the houses?"), centered on the adverb *nósphi* 'apart, away, aloof' that punctuates the successive stages of Demeter's retreat.[15]

Finally, Demeter retreats inside her own temple, and nothing more grows on the land. To annihilate (*phthîsai*) men already requires some reflection, but to reduce the honors owed to the immortals to nothing, that is the greatest threat! Therefore, all of Zeus's effort, like that of the Achaeans with Achilles, is directed toward putting "an end to

[12] *Homeric Hymn to Demeter* 91–93.

[13] She is not only chaste, like women mourning at the Thesmophoria the day of the *Nēsteía* (see F. Zeitlin, "Cultic Models of the Female: Rites of Dionysus and Demeter," *Arethusa* 15 [1982]: 149), but beyond maternity.

[14] The original isolation is indeed Zeus's doing, who acts *nósphi mētrós* (lines 4 and 72, with Richardson's commentary on line 4, and Segal, "Orality, Repetition, and Formulaic Artistry," 132–34 n. 108). Demeter only returns Zeus's gesture.

[15] *Homeric Hymn to Demeter* 113–17, 302–4. On *nósphi*, see P. Chantraine, *Dictionnaire étymologique de la langue grecque* (Paris, 1968–1980), s.v.

the terrible wrath" of the goddess against the immortals.[16] And, just as with Achilles, just as with Coriolanus, embassies hasten to Demeter without success. Zeus insists, however, and for a good reason: it is he who did everything, he who has, at any rate, wished everything—is he not in this matter the universal father, of gods, of men, and of Persephone, whom he has given to Hades without her mother's permission? Zeus has *wished* everything, and it is he again finally, in the infinite indulgence of the all-powerful, who "will want" to agree to the reconciliation of the goddess with the gods.[17] But if the text recognizes to its fullest the initiative of the decision of the Father, we can also see very clearly that it is the wrath of Demeter that wins the game: because up to this point, all attempts were fruitless, beginning with the sending of the messenger Iris, and ending with all the gods filing past in turn. And Demeter always says *no* (*enaíneto, ou . . . pote pháske*). This "no" is conditional, however (I will *not* yield, *not before* I see my daughter with my own eyes),[18] since Demeter is not as resourceless as a mortal mother, and since she knows she can find Persephone, and so there is an opportunity for reconciliation. There is time for Hermes to go and come back from Hades, and the mother finds her daughter again. Then, for the reconciliation to take place, Zeus still has to send Rhea, their common mother, to Demeter, who thinks of the goddess as her mother particularly.

(In passing, I do wonder about mothers: Rhea alone can reconcile Demeter and Zeus, Thetis alone can convince Achilles to give Hector's body back to Priam, and Coriolanus's mother alone can prevent him from attacking Rome. Is the resemblance between these three embassies coincidental? Or should we detect in it an admission—so scattered throughout the texts that we have to look for it—of a "political" power of mothers, in the sense that there is nothing more political in Greek thought than a reconciliation? This certainly goes against

---

[16] *Homeric Hymn to Demeter* 338–39, 349–50, and 410.

[17] *Boulé* or *mêtis* of Zeus: lines 9, 30, 414–15; Zeus as responsible (*aítios*): 77–78; Zeus father: 21, 27, 415; his goodwill: 445.

[18] For example, lines 331–33. See C. Wooten, "The Conditional Nature of *prin* Clauses in Attic Prose of the Fifth and Fourth Century," *Glotta* 48 (1970): 81–88.

the public mistrust of mothers we thought we had uncovered . . . A question to pursue.)

All is well that ends well, then, in the *Homeric Hymn to Demeter*. The reconciliation is made on Demeter's terms, and it is obviously an optimistic version of the episode. There are other versions that are less so: thus the Arcadian *lógos* about the black Demeter, the one about Demeter Erinys (the Arcadian way of designating a furious Demeter), which ascribes the goddess's wrath to the abduction of Persephone but, without mentioning the happy reunion between mother and daughter, assigns to Demeter unconditional appeasement.[19] Certainly the goddess receives a cult as an offering, as if to offset her loss;[20] but because there is nothing that can compensate for the loss of a child, the Arcadian cult celebrates her mourning as a black woman, her wrath as an Erinys. The Mother of the gods—still called Mother or Great Mother—is also rewarded with a ritual and with the same silence about the lost child's whereabouts in a famous chorus of Euripides: the chorus mentions her *póthos,* her burning desire in the form of the regrets she feels for "the young woman who has gone, whose name is unspoken"; her mourning that cannot be forgotten (*pénthos álaston*), and her black wrath (*stugíous orgás, mênin Matrós*), erased by her laughter as soon as she hears the sound of the tambourine. And the Mother, enticed by the ritual cries, takes the flute . . .[21] An exchange indeed has taken place: the goddess is rid of—

---

[19] *Melaina:* Pausanias 8.42.1–5; Erinys: Pausanias 8.25.6; cf. M. Jost, *Sanctuaires et cultes d'Arcadie* (Paris, 1985), 314. Must we conclude concerning Demeter's not obtaining anything in Phigalia that this is "the vocation of a mother who is terrible at reconciliation" ("vocation de la mère terrible à se réconcilier"), as P. Lévêque does, in *Colère, sexe, rire: Le Japon des mythes anciens* (Paris, 1988), 41–44?

[20] Similarly, as G. Cerri notes ("La Madre dei Dei nell' *Elena* di Euripide: Tragedia e rituale," *Quaderni di storia* 18 [1983]: 155–95, especially p. 181), it is at the end of her wanderings, and not at the time of her reunion with Kore that the Eleusinian Demeter establishes the mysteries.

[21] Euripides *Helen* 1300–1352. We should note that the *Homeric Hymn to Demeter* knows very well the laughter of the goddess responding to the devotee Iambe and her gestures (lines 200–204; cf. M. Olender, "Aspects de *Baubô*: Textes et contextes antiques," *Revue de l'histoire des religions* 202 [1985]; Olender establishes the link at p. 22 n. 85), but this is only a stage of the story, not the last one by any means, and we

exalláxat(e), says Zeus to the Charites—her sorrow, which has been replaced by laughter; after this exchange, she only has to establish the ritual in all meekness. But it is possible that this exchange is inequitable for a mother, even though divine, since the beloved daughter, the object of sorrow, also disappears silently from the story, alongside sorrow itself.[22]

To bring this list of great maternal wraths to an end, I would evoke the *mênis* of Achilles' mother as Laura Slatkin has reconstructed it, which finds here both its model and its confirmation: the wrath of a goddess who is forced to marry a mortal man without compensation; the grief of Thetis mourning a son who is about to die; the grief-wrath of Thetis, who knows that "the price of Zeus' hegemony is Achilles' death" and who forces Zeus to give in because he knows she knows. Because Homer has displaced the wrath from a mother to her son, and because the maternal *mênis* "becomes absorbed in the actual wrath of her son,"[23] we credit the hero with a Great Mother's wrath without seeing that mourning and wrath are undivided between the mother and the son. Yet it is necessary to give back to Thetis what makes the *Iliad* Achilles' poem . . .

More cruel yet than the fate of divine mothers in tragedy is that of mortal women: whether triumphant or heartbroken queens, they are always wounded in their motherhood. From that moment when mothers obtain only the horrified sight of the child's corpse to compensate for their loss, mourning that has already been transformed into wrath becomes vengeance in deeds. And mothers kill. They put

---

must speak of a *pause* in mourning rather than of the "conclusion of divine mourning" ("dénouement du deuil divin": Olender 21), unless we think that the process of conclusion "inaugurates itself" truly at this precise moment.

[22] On this particular point, I disagree with Cerri "La Madre dei Dei," 156–57), who concludes about the "fusion" between Demeter and the Mother of the gods in this text that, outside of the narrative, the end of the story would be the same as that at Eleusis; nothing, however, allows us to make up for Euripides' silence on this point, and it is this silence that we should question.

[23] Slatkin, "The Wrath of Thetis," 22.

the guilty man to death—always a man, and sometimes children, the culprit's sons.

Let us consider Hecuba again, in Euripides' play of the same name. Her whole being has suffered because of Polyxena's death, but it is the mutilated corpse of Polydorus that leads her to vengeance. She asks Agamemnon for the assistance of law, which he incarnates and protects: an avenging law, which is less that of blood than that of justice, armed against those who kill their hosts. When the king shirks his duty, caring little to be seen in the Greek army's eyes as the avenger (*timōrós*) of a Trojan woman, Hecuba takes action: she asks for help from Vengeance itself and from the race of women united against males in the service of the mother. Hecuba then acts: she performs a woman's *érgon;*[24] and if the Trojan women who kill with pins are "bitches" for Polymestor, it would be a good idea to keep in mind that a female dog is an Erinys only because she is complete motherhood.[25] Later on, moreover, Hecuba will become a bitch on the boat taking her to Greece. The mourning mother has fulfilled her fate.

There is also Clytemnestra, *mênis* personified, whom Aeschylus puts in charge of memory (*mnámōn mênis*); Clytemnestra, who is too easily made into an adulterer and who is all resentment on account of the murder of Iphigenia, which was badly masqueraded as a sacrifice. Clytemnestra, then, will kill the culprit with her own hand: the husband who knew not how to be a father.[26]

Some clarification is needed here: Demeter, the Mother of the gods, and Clytemnestra are mothers whose daughters have been taken away

[24] *Eirgasai: Hecuba* 1122; feminine *érgon*: Loraux, *Experiences of Tiresias*, 245–46. *Timōrós: Hecuba* 789–90, 842–43; the race of women against men: 883–87 (Danaids and Lemnian women), 1177–84.

[25] Female dogs: *Hecuba* 1173 (*miaiphónous kúnas*); Hecuba as a bitch: 1265–73. In the *Iambics on Women* (Semonides of Amorgos frag. 7 West), the bitch is *autométōr* (line 12), "motherhood personified."

[26] *Mnámōn mênis teknópoinos* 'memory's servant, wrath that wants to avenge a child': Aeschylus *Agamemnon* 155. Clytemnestra is "adulterous bitch," certainly, but also "bitch enraged by her daughter's murder"; see J.-G. Trilling's remarks in "James Joyce ou l'écriture matricide," *Études freudiennes* 7–8 (1973): 68.

or killed. Demeter the goddess finds Kore and is reconciled—what else can the Mistress of grain do when the black Erinyes themselves have been reconciled with Athens, and when the Great Mother herself has exchanged her sorrow for mystic laughter? Mortal, Clytemnestra knows death in her daughter: she has irremediably lost Iphigenia, whom no Artemis brings to Tauris in Aeschylus, and she kills the murderous father. Because of her daughter, and not because of her lover, it bears repeating, because Aeschylus's text is transparent on this point.

Thus Clytemnestra joins the tragic cohort of women murderers, with this exception—and this is not a small point: these mothers are often murderers who, like Medea, kill their own children better to destroy their husbands. But then they always kill sons, hence depriving their spouse of the arrogant tranquillity of a father whose sons will perpetuate his name and lineage. It is not that these heartbroken mothers kill the children to whom they gave birth, but because the father annexed them to his own power, they thereby destroy the father in the husband.[27]

If Freud had been less preoccupied with Oedipus and more observant of Medea when he remarked that aggression "forms the basis of every relation of affection and love among people," he would certainly not have added: "with the single exception, perhaps, of the mother's relation to her male child."[28] Blindness on the part of the inventor of "Oedipus"? Perhaps. Be that as it may, the tragic thinking of the Greeks places mothers in a dreadful ambivalence, where wrath against spouse prevails over the bodily intimacy with the child. Intimacy is first, and wrath is second: why should the latter get the better of the former?

Unless we should postulate an archetypal wrath against men, archaic and always unspoken . . . I would rather not set out on the path

---

[27] The reasoning of Euripides' Medea is perfectly clear from this standpoint; see *Medea* 792–96, 803–4, 816–17, 1056–58, etc.

[28] S. Freud, *Civilization and Its Discontents* (New York, 1962), 60. In light of such a claim, we understand better Freud's silence concerning the mother of Richard III (see p. 6 above and note 6).

of little-supported hypotheses, especially since in this case it is less a matter of speculating on the actual feelings of mothers than on those that men, at the same time fascinated with the feminine and afraid of women, ascribe to the woman they consider fulfilled, the one who is both wife *and* mother.

It is best to stick to the text, and to note that vengeance does not follow the same course whether the mother has a son or a daughter for a child. This observation can be expressed in the form of a couple of rules:

1. A mother never kills a daughter,[29] even when this daughter is named Electra and mother and daughter hate each other from the bottom of their hearts;[30] but a mother whose husband has killed a daughter will in turn kill the guilty father—this is Clytemnestra again.

2. A murderous mother always kills her son(s), because the important thing is to get at the husband who as a father is guilty of—outside of other, often serious, grievances—having compromised and destroyed the intimate relationship with the child.

But the rules explain themselves, especially when, after the fact, they shed some light on what precedes: let us bear in mind that the daughter could be designated as ōdís, a word that refers to the act of childbirth, in its length and in its pain, just before the separation between mother and child is accomplished; the son could be said to be the lókheuma, the finished product of childbirth, already separate from the mother, already ready to be "civilized" by paternal recogni-

---

[29] With the exception of Praxithea, who only agrees to the killing of her daughter in a sacrifice that, far from being a *míasma* like that of Iphigenia sacrificed by her own father (*Agamemnon* 209; cf. 220), saves Athens. But if the queen is a model, it is less certain that the mother is.

[30] "La gamme des crimes concevables: meurtre du père, du fils, du mari, non de la fille" ("The gamut of imaginable crimes: murder of the father, of the son, of the husband, not of the daughter"), thus Vidal-Naquet, *Tragédies* 31 (preface to Aeschylus). To a theatergoer in Strasbourg, who marveled at Clytemnestra's not going so far as to take the plunge, I would offer these reminders: (1) in Sophocles, the murder plan against Electra is clearly attributed to Aegisthus (*Electra* 379–82, 386, 389); (2) in Euripides, it is Clytemnestra herself who protects her daughter from her lover (*Electra* 23–30).

tion. Is it a coincidence, then, that Praxithea, for whom daughters are a substitute for sons, called her daughters *lokheúmata*—that is, in the service of and at the disposition of the citizens?

Thus we come to the astounding scene in the *Homeric Hymn to Demeter*[31] in which a divine mother comes face to face with a mortal one, with this extra detail: the divine mother has a daughter whereas the mortal woman gave birth to a beloved son. At Celeus's court in Eleusis, Demeter, in the reassuring shape of an old nurse, wants to immortalize the child Demophon, who has been duly anointed by her with ambrosia and hidden in the fire. "She would have saved him from old age and death, without Metaneira's folly, who, watching her during the night, saw her from her fragrant room." Panic of the mortal mother who cries just as if over a dead body (*kókusen*) and, "frightened for her son, strikes her own thighs." Wrath of the divine nurse, who pushes the child away from her onto the ground where human beings walk. Demophon will not be immortal, and, notwithstanding his pitiful cries, he has to relearn his condition as mortal child. Metaneira is said to be "crazy" and "lost." And in fact, she did make a serious mistake of interpretation when she prematurely started to mourn[32] a child whom Demeter was saving from the life of mortals. It is possible, moreover, that she has already symbolically condemned her son to death with her thoughtless gesture: by striking her thighs, she not only expresses the sharp grief she feels, as is usually claimed, but she also repeats the gesture with which Ares and then Patroclus vow to die the death of a warrior in the *Iliad*.[33] Clearly it is not her own life that the mother abandons in a moment of madness

---

[31] *Homeric Hymn to Demeter* 233–62. From the perspective of applied psychoanalysis, M. Arthur ("Politics and Pomegranates") gives a very different interpretation of the scene between the mothers.

[32] *Homeric Hymn to Demeter* 247: *olophuroméne;* 249: *góon kaì kēdéa lugrá;* 250: *oduroméne.* As a matter of fact, there are other, less edifying, versions of the story in which Demophon actually dies: see Richardson at 254 (references) and G. Nagy, *Pindar's Homer* (Baltimore, 1990).

[33] *Homeric Hymn to Demeter* 245; S. Lowenstam analyzes the gesture of Patroclus and Ares in *The Death of Patroklos: A Study in Typology* (Königstein, 1981), 59–60, 100, 164.

(unconsciously, if we want to understand it so), but the life of a cherished son. The gentle Metaneira has deprived Demophon of immortality; she has "killed" him. And Demeter can leave again to go into retreat, entirely given over to her grief over her daughter.

Is it really hazardous for a son to have a mother, and for a mother to have a son?

It is a strange journey that leads from everyday funerals in which the role of mothers is as limited as possible outside of the house, to murderous mothers; a strange journey indeed that proceeds from mothers begging to get their sons' bodies back for a last embrace toward mothers who protect their daughters and kill their sons. Before worrying about such obviously drastic reversals, however, we should remember that the materials of the inquiry belong to different registers. There are the civic regulations intended to diminish the risks in daily life, and then there are the scenes of lamentation that tragedy can develop well beyond what would be allowed in the real-life city: there the weeping mothers are allowed to form a chorus and to establish their sorrow in the theater, on the condition that they weep over those warriors who are presented as so many model citizens by Adrastus in his eulogy. In this way, tragedy takes some liberties with respect to norms, but, for the most part, orthodoxy is not damaged. A decisive step is taken with goddesses, because the Great Mothers do not need any authorization to engage in mourning, a mourning that is necessary to them—indeed is it not, to a large extent, an actual component of their being, in forms that run the gamut, in the spectrum of extreme grief, from *álaston pénthos* ('mourning that cannot forget') to *mênis*? It then becomes clear that those black Mothers, who are fearsome to the same degree that they are mourning, are weeping over daughters whom men (fathers) have taken away from them. We need only to leave epic and hymnic poetry, where mothers are divine, for tragedy, where they are queens and mortal, and the observation becomes obvious: the human condition, as presented in myth and later in tragedy, is cruel; death is the unavoidable end, and nothing will ever offset mourning. Therefore, grief that is too strong takes action, and this, in the tragic mode, means murder. Clytemnestra kills Agamemnon for the love of Iphigenia, but she will not kill Electra; Medea kills her beloved sons because of Jason. In tragedy, the tension between the sexes is strong, and the woman affected by *páthos* always turns against men. In accordance with the tradition of the "race of women"—which the *ándres* rouse when they want to feel both terror and fascination—the mother lives with her daughter in a closed circle, but feminine wrath threatens the son, because he stands in for the father.

Under the sign of taking action, everything is redistributed, and since the new order is fantastical, it enjoys its own coherence. Alongside the Lemnian women and the husband-killing Danaids, the murderous mother of a son haunts, therefore, the fantasies of terror that Greek men experience when they face the race of women. Yet this dreadful mother takes the poetic form of a paradigm,[34] the paradigm of the nightingale who was a mother and sings the double loss of having killed the son she loved, and who weeps over both her bereavement and her act. As if murder and mourning came under one and the same logic for the mother of a male child. Things become more complicated, though, because the mourning nightingale is also the symbol of all feminine despair, be it that of a mother or not. As if there were only one model for all mourning women: at the same time maternal *and* desperately deadly.

We can guess the consequences of such a configuration: it suggests that all feminine mourning may be less wound or anger than remorse. Is a woman in tears originally guilty of whatever makes her cry? Doubtless the *ándres* have found a justification for the civic gesture that keeps women apart in this completely imaginary—and, as we

---

[34] Here I agree with Piero Pucci, whose study on the nightingale, presented in March 1989 within the framework of research done under the auspices of the EHESS, also speaks of a "paradigm." There is some divergence in purpose between Pucci's analysis, which I encountered only after I finished a first draft of this text, and mine, but also a great deal of convergence in our interpretation of the relevant passages.

shall see, very largely tragic—construction: if every woman imitates a deviant mother with her tears,[35] it is an elegant—theatrical—way of putting the mother out of play, insofar as she would be a very ambivalent paradigm of mourning.

The moral of the story, at least as it was told in Megara, requires that the cruel mother die of weeping over her fate and her act:

> The women [Procne and Philomela] came to Athens, and while they sang their lament about what they suffered and what they did in revenge (*thrēnoûsai hoîa épathon kaì hoîa antédrasan*),[36] they died because of their tears.
>
> (Pausanias 1.41.9)

However much Pausanias insists—with his unrepentant rationalism—that the metamorphoses of Procne and Philomela into nightingale and swallow reflect only the characteristics of the song of those birds, which is "mournful and similar to a *thrênos*," there is no one in all the ancient audiences of tragedy who would not have known that any nightingale who sings may just as well—and beautifully—be a Procne who cries.

[35] It goes without saying that the psychic operation thus described presupposes a civic organization in which women are kept out of the political sphere and men no longer cry, unlike the epic heroes studied by Hélène Monsacré in *Les larmes d'Achille* (Paris, 1984).

[36] Let us bear in mind that *patheîn* and *drân* are the two verbs of tragic action; as for the *thrênos,* it is consubstantial with the nightingale to such a degree that we even find the verb *thrēneîn* in Aristophanes *Birds* 211.

Mourning Nightingale

Dear to tragedy because it is tied to the great Athenian myths, the story is well known in its basic details. Although Sophocles' tragedy about Procne[1] has survived only in fragments, mythographers have repeatedly told the tale: how Tereus, king of Thrace—even though a semibarbarian—marries Procne, daughter of the Athenian king, and how, after his wife begs him because she misses her sister Philomela so much, he goes back to Athens to fetch his sister-in-law; then how, on the way back, he rapes Philomela and, to prevent her from accusing him, cuts off her tongue; how Philomela is able to tell the story by weaving the events into a fabric; how Procne understands what happened, and, with the help of her hapless sister, kills Itys, her child by Tereus. Tereus in turn becomes a hoopoe who endlessly pursues Procne-the-nightingale and Philomela-the-swallow.[2]

---

[1] The tragedy was probably called *Tereus,* but, despite all his efforts to give an important role to Tereus in the story, N. C. Hourmouziades notes that most of the plot revolves around the feminine solidarity between Procne, Philomela, and a chorus of women ("Sophocles' Tereus," in *Studies in Honor of T. B. L. Webster* [Bristol, 1986], 134–42).

[2] In the Latin poets and in the Renaissance tradition, the roles are exchanged, and it is Philomela who becomes a nightingale: the nightingale from here on does not

In the *Odyssey,* the murderous mother is not (not yet?) called Procne, but simply Aedon (Nightingale). Mother of an only son, she is jealous of her sister-in-law, herself a prolific mother, who is named, as we would expect, Niobe. The rest of the story is easily guessed. Nightingale cannot refrain from killing her rival's eldest son. But we know that Niobe's children, sacrificed to another rivalry between mothers, have been consecrated to the arrows of Apollo and Artemis. During the night, Nightingale mistakenly kills her own son Itylos. We will perhaps be tempted to muse upon the convergence, which is only implicit in the Homeric text, between the nightingale and the weeping rock, between two mothers, one jealous, the other too proud, who both ultimately kill their own child, whether with their own hands or not . . . This is the proof, if proof were needed, that mothers with sons are dangerous not only to their children but also to themselves.

We will forget here—as the tragedians always do when they evoke Procne—everything that is not mother and child. With Tereus and Philomela out of mind, the murder of Itys and the *thrēnos* of Procne remain—the woman's crying and the nightingale's song are impossible to separate. Murder is a woman's crime and counts as one of the model feminine crimes: as such, murder is worthy of appearing in the tragic catalogues of *gunaikeîa érga* that choruses recite from time to time. After Heracles kills his own son in a fit of madness, the chorus evokes both the husband-killing Danaids and Procne, murderer of Itys, in order to conclude, in each case, that a father's crime outdoes all imaginable transgressions.[3] Here is the murder of Itys:

---

weep over a son, but over a rape. Thus, in the last chapter of the *Songe de Poliphile* (by F. Colonna, 1467), Philomela "laments the violence of the adulterous and perfid Tereus, singing: *Tēreús, Tēreús, emè ebiásato*"; and, in Shakespeare's *Rape of Lucrece,* the evocation of the nightingale is a response to the polluted wife's cries ("Come, Philomela, that sing'st of ravishment"). The paradigm is completely transformed.

[3] A father does not kill his son, even in tragedy, unless he is seized by a fit of madness like Heracles: see Aristotle *Poetics* 1453b19–22 for a list of possible crimes (see Loraux, "La guerra nella famiglia," 5–35, 21).

> Of the wretched noble son of
> Procne—mother only once—I can say
> his murder was a sacrifice to the Muses.
>
> (Euripides *Heracles* 1021–23)

And the chorus adds:

> But you, you have fathered three children, cruel one,
> and you killed them in your madness.
>
> (Euripides *Heracles* 1024–25)

A sacrifice to the Muses?[4] So be it, since the mother's mourning has been transformed into melodious song. In fact, it was especially important to mention the incommensurable horror of Heracles the infanticide.

The nightingale is more often evoked in the context of feminine lament, and as a figure emblematic of it. Thus, in Aeschylus's *Suppliant Women,* we find the nightingale represented in the chorus of Danaids, who, crying over their own fate, imagine that a seer clever at interpreting bird songs would hear in their lament the voice of "Tereus's wife of the pitiful deceit"—that is, the voice of the nightingale. And they will sing the painful song of Procne-nightingale, who, historian of her own life,[5] recounts the child's death, victim of a "bad mother's wrath."[6]

Danaos's daughters can be identified with Procne because they cry; they do not know yet—but a tragedian, playing with myths to transform one into the past of the other, knows—that they themselves will soon commit another one of the great feminine crimes. What compels those virgins, who are so keen on their own integrity, to

[4] For commentary on this passage, I refer to Pucci's analysis, which I hope will be published soon.

[5] The verb *xuntíthēsi* (line 4) is the one that Thucydides, for example, uses to refer to the composition of his history.

[6] Aeschylus *Suppliant Women* 57–66; on mourning suppliant women, see lines 111–16; for the recurrent bird metaphor, lines 223–24, 226.

compare their lament to a mother's mourning? Aeschylus does not offer an answer to this question, nor does any other tragedian, except in action: on stage, there is not a single mother who invokes this model by its proper name, and for a very good reason: why would a mother adopt a paradigm that incorporates murder in mourning? And the only mother (Ajax's) who may evoke for others the "song of the pitiful nightingale" is supposed to reject it for a more piercing death-cry, the cry *aílinos,* this ritual scansion of the blows that mourning women inflict on their bodies.[7] The paradox here is that it is virgins or wives who call on the maternal paradigm, as if all feminine roles, with the exception of that of a mother, can be explained by referring to the figure of the nightingale.[8]

Let us go back to Penelope. She is a mother, to be sure, but first and foremost she is a wife, and it is her husband she weeps over during her long sleepless nights; her immeasurable mourning (*amétrēton*) evokes the figure of Aedon, "mourning her son Itylos, whom she killed with the bronze long ago, in a moment of madness." Certainly, when she finally comments on the relationship between her fate and the nightingale's, Penelope confesses that she worries because her son is pressing her to leave her house for a new husband; but even though he is missing, it is Odysseus who is in the queen's thoughts, and it is her vacillation between her husband's rights and the demands of the present that connects her with the nightingale.[8]

From this point on, the nightingale will be evoked only in tragedy and by or with regard to young women. There are the Danaids, Electra and Antigone, and then Cassandra. Cassandra is a nightingale for the elders in the *Agamemnon,* because when she sings a bitter lament over herself, they think of the tawny bird who never tires of her cry when she moans: "Itys! Itys!" But Cassandra rejects the com-

---

[7] *Ajax* 627–628; we should note, however, that (1) Ajax is not dead, but mad; (2) it is the chorus who ascribes this refusal to Periboe; (3) a tragic virgin also happens to refuse the comparison that the chorus applies to her, and it is Cassandra.

[8] *Odyssey* 19.511–34, a perfectly coherent passage that we need not declare an interpolation, as so many experts on Homer have done.

parison, because, rather than meeting death, the nightingale receives a bird's body from the gods; Cassandra's situation is different: "For me remains the destruction of the two-edged sword."[9] Thus Cassandra rejects the paradigm, and no other allusion will be made to the myth except for the name of Itys, which is also—which perhaps is only—the bird's cry: Cassandra is going to die, and she sees Procne, who remains unnamed, in every nightingale. Because of the dreadful visions that possess her, the inspired seer cares little for the codified images of tragedy. Elegiac lament is not for her.

For Electra, on the other hand, only the nightingale can come close to her grief—and she appeals to the bird twice,[10] referring to "the bird who laments 'Itys,' always 'Itys'!" and then evoking—should we be surprised?—Niobe, "the all-suffering, who, in her grave of stone, alas, weeps." That she claims Niobe as a tutelary divinity perhaps suggests a new rule: this daughter, who fiercely mourns her father, seems to find mythological equivalents only in stories of murderous mothers.

But in relating Niobe to the nightingale, Electra not only confirms the paradigm; she makes everything more complex. Certainly, she does not relent from associating, with great cool, the tears she sheds for a murdered father and the lament of Nightingale, "children-killer," and it is difficult to determine whether this comparison is as appropriate as Electra claims it is, or whether, on the contrary, it is as immediately irrelevant as the evocation of Procne by the Danaids. We should note at any rate the degree to which the repetitive *aeí* of mourning is consubstantial to her (*aeí* of the nightingale, with, in the case of Niobe, the echo of an *aiaî* 'alas'), because, much farther on in the play, the chorus describes her as "always (*aeí*) moaning miserably over her father, like the nightingale, all lament." But Sophocles' subtlety may suggest much more about Electra's taste for the figure of the

---

[9] *Agamemnon* 1140–49.

[10] Sophocles *Electra* 107 (as a nightingale who has killed her children), 147–49; and, at 1075, the chorus compares her to the nightingale. The relevance of the comparison is made clear at 147 by the verb *ararískō*, which explains the specific analogy. Niobe: 150–52.

"distraught" bird who was a murderous mother: Electra seems to be secretly fascinated by the idea of a mother who kills—this murderous mother who Clytemnestra has precisely not been for her but would probably have liked to have been for Orestes. As if Electra mourning her father killed by Clytemnestra were dreaming of a mother who would kill her instead of Agamemnon—but Clytemnestra obstinately denies the hateful pleasure Electra would enjoy anticipating her own death by maternal blows. Unless in her endless mourning Agamemnon's daughter is "mending" the image of the mother, finding here again what was Clytemnestra's truth—the despair over sacrificed Iphigenia. In this case, Electra will find in her own grief the very loss that Clytemnestra made Agamemnon pay for with the price of blood, and, by weeping over the death of her father and by moaning over him, Electra repeats the lament of the mother she thought she had rejected . . . How can we decide where tragedy remains silent? I will refrain from doing so. In any case, by adopting the feminine paradigm of the crying mother, Electra says much about her own ambivalence toward a mother who has only hate to proclaim.

Thus it is fitting to explain further what has been asserted about the nightingale paradigm. It is clear that a mother never appeals to it, while virgins display a strange predilection for referring to it. We should also add that because of the incongruence inherent in using this paradigm, the tragedians, each in his own way, take pains to suggest some hidden affinity between the speaker and the figure that she adopts. Like Procne, the Danaids will kill, and Electra's hatred for her mother conceals more than a simple and quiet rejection. As for Antigone . . .

Antigone also believes she most closely resembles Niobe,[11] but when she despairs before the naked corpse of Polynices, the guard sees and hears in her the bird that shrieks at the sight of an empty nest, empty of her young.[12] Perhaps, as some suggest, Sophocles is thinking here of the wrathful eagles from the *parodos* in the *Agamemnon;* we

---

[11] Sophocles *Antigone* 825–33 (Niobe): "most similar" (*homoiotátan*).
[12] *Antigone* 423–428.

should keep in mind that the allusion to the bird is very vague, even though the identification with Niobe is developed at length.[13] The fact remains that Antigone is compared to a mother,[14] and that Euripides does not hesitate in the least to decode the allusion. In this way he attributes to his own Antigone an explicit identification with the mother who has only one son, whom she has lost, the mother who cries through the songbird:

> Wretched me, as the cry is raised!
> What bird, sitting on the highest branches of an oak
> or a fir-tree, mother only once, with her moans
> will sing together with me over my sorrows?[15]
>
> (Euripides *Phoenician Women* 1514–18)

In this case, Antigone weeps over three corpses—her mother's and her two brothers'. But the rest of her lament says it all: like a Homeric mourner, she weeps in advance over her future life. In Euripides, who is always preoccupied with unexpected reversals, yet deeply faithful to tragic rules, Antigone weeps over a mother and her children but identifies herself, a virgin, with the nightingale.

In young women's tears is the mourning and despair of a murderess, less incongruent than it first appears, once it is put back in its dramatic context, and always paradigmatic of all feminine lament. Is it neces-

---

[13] Although a long tradition gives a maternal connotation to this image, from the desperate bird in book 2 of the *Iliad* (311–15): "The mother fluttered around them, lamenting over her dear children," *mētēr d'amphepotâto oduroménē phíla tékna*, to Gregory of Nazianzus's eloquent description of the mother of young martyrs who refuses to lament "as a bird over her nestlings" (*hōs neossoùs órnis,* Migne 35.926a = *Oratio* 15 [*In Machabaeorum Laudem*]); on the "negative lament" developed in Gregory of Nazianzus 928a–b, see Alexiou, *Ritual Lament,* 32–33.

[14] On the relationship between Oedipus's daughter and her mother, Jocasta, see N. Loraux, "La main d'Antigone," *Mètis* 1 (1986): 194–95.

[15] *Elelízō* (line 1514) is the verb that denotes the nightingale's song: see, for example, *Helen* 112. *Monomátōr* should not be translated "mother bereft of her young"; I see here an allusion to the *monotéknou* of *Heracles* 1022: the nightingale then has been "mother only once."

sary to decode the imprint of hate in this configuration? As if one really mourns for having *destroyed* and not only for having lost.[16]

Or, more precisely, as if, to avert mothers' tears, it were *necessary* to make mothers criminals. Since all womanly tears must be guilty tears, since female mourning is suspicious, and since a mother's mourning, like that in *Richard III,* contains all the others, suspicion must hang over maternal tears. Such a thought process is fruitful: a subtle decoder of feminine secrets, discovering (rediscovering) this hate (placed there by a long-lasting tradition of male thinking),[17] would see his mistrust of women's mourning justified by the excess of grief and by the exasperating repetition of the *aeí.*

As a result, love thus liberated passes over to the side of the *ándres.* And, as in Pericles' funeral oration, as at the end of Aeschylus's *Eumenides,* all of the citizens' love is for the city.

This could be the last word of the story, and we could well decide that it is actually the last word.

All in all, the construction seems complete, since the decoding of these representations supports what the study of funeral laws has suggested. It is the same embarrassment or the same muffled anxiety that becomes clear in the institutional gesture as well as in the thought operation that fantasizes maternal mourning into a threat. With the exception that this thought process does not let itself, has not let itself, be understood in one moment only. We must attempt to find our bearings on shaky ground by patiently distinguishing stages and periods, because claims that are too obvious are doomed to be refuted, or at any rate displaced or denied. Thus the sensual proximity of the mother to her son's body required that the corpse that mothers long for be a son's body: this is much too extreme a vision, because it is definitely too eroticized. This road must be blocked: thus Theseus will at all costs forbid mothers the sight of sons who have died in war.

---

[16] A preliminary sketch of this idea has appeared in the *Nouvelle revue de psychanalyse* 34 (1986): 253–57.

[17] "Hearsay of men" (*phátis andrõn*) that is the source of her knowledge about Niobe, according to Antigone's own confession (*Antigone* 829).

But a true reversal obtrudes to correct this first claim: here is the Mother par excellence who is the mother of a cherished daughter, in the closed circle of the race of women; this allows her to return against the son all the hostility that is reasonably postulated among mothers. And the mother will kill males: sometimes her husband, more generally her son. The civic imagination can now draw the conclusion hoped for from the beginning: there can be no innocence behind mourning and feminine tears because a woman is always the cause of her own tears.

Curtain.

There is, nevertheless, an epilogue.

Whatever satisfaction we may expect to gain from a construction carried through to a successful conclusion, I cannot bring myself to accept this conclusion as good. It is far too simple: by sticking to the main directions drawn so far, we would eventually come to believe in the realization of the male fantasy. As a result, Greek mothers would in fact be dangerous, and women would never be excluded from the city so much as when they are mothers. In everyday life, however, it is clear that this is not what happens in cities: the civic community loves calm too much to risk such a direct confrontation with representations that are more prudently kept in a latent state, so as to put both fear and fascination at a good distance. In the latent state, this thought of the feminine is at the same time obliterated and available but no longer threatens to invade unexpectedly the civic stage.

The stage is taken over peacefully by a system of representations much more reassuring for the good functioning of the political sphere, insofar as it allows everything to be done as if one actually trusted mothers.

Moreover, the Great Mother is in the Agora of Athens, in a position that could not be more official. This is the proof that she is lastingly appeased.

Totally appeased? Perhaps. Whatever the case, it is necessary to investigate.

The Mother in the Agora

In the Athenian agora, a place both centered in the present and highly symbolic of the political as democracy understands it, was a temple of the Mother, a temple of the Mother of the gods, to be more precise. This mother seems to have been virtually generic, though some of the evidence says that she was identical with Rhea, if not with Demeter—the same Demeter who is celebrated at Eleusis. But the Mother should be opposed to Demeter, "as nature is to culture."[1]

The origin of this temple of the Mother—the Metroon—whose location has been identified by American excavations,[2] is explained in an *aition* supported by a long tradition, though we may well hesitate to treat this account as historical evidence. If, however, we care about symbolical meaning, it is worthwhile to listen to the tale as it was told in the fourth century A.D. by the emperor Julian, a devout follower of

[1] The Metroon, sanctuary of Rhea: scholia on Aeschines *Against Ctesiphon* 187; Arrian *Periplous* 9; Julian *Discourse* 5 (*To the Mother of the Gods*), 159a. Demeter and the Great Mother: H. A. Thompson, "Building on the West Side of the Agora," *Hesperia* 6 (1937): 205–6 (which overstates the relationship by erasing the difference between mysteries open to all and the orgies of the Great Mother, which some say were celebrated only by women). Nature and culture: Cerri, "La Madre dei Dei," 157–58.

[2] On the Metroon, see Thompson, "Building on the West Side of the Agora," 135–217.

the Great Mother.[3] Julian relates how the Athenians insulted and chased—other versions say killed—the Gallus, priest of the Mother, "without understanding the importance of the goddess"; how they thus incurred the *mênis* of the Mother; how they tried to appease her wrath by consulting the Pythia at Delphi, who ordered them to build the Metroon. A cult to appease the *mênis* of a divine mother? The theme is well known to us, but the location of the temple in the heart of the city is quite remarkable.

During the fourth century, the Metroon was located next to the Bouleuterion, seat of the Athenian Council, or Boule, which was responsible for the proper functioning of the democracy: the Boule initiated many decrees, and the *stratēgoí* could be heard there. And it was in the Boule that each tenth of a year, a tenth of the Council (a prytany) watched over the meetings of the Assembly of citizens. What should be made of the proximity between the seat of the Council and the temple of the Mother of the gods? That gods may play the part of "citizens,"[4] perhaps! But what of the wild Mother who speeds across mountains, first surrendering entirely to mourning, then to the joy of the ritual? In what sense of the word *pólis* can she be said to be "political"? It may be precisely because she has agreed to put an end to her *mênis.* Such an explanation would obviously not be satisfactory to positivist historians, who would rather explain the closeness of the sanctuary and the Bouleuterion by appealing to contingency or, at best, to simple convenience: if the Council sat in the temple at the beginning, it is because the members of the Boule found there the large room they needed, they say. This is, certainly, very far from being an organic link.[5] I confess that I am not in the least convinced by these "practical" arguments, which, as is often the case, do not really explain anything. And when the dying orator Lycurgus asked to be carried to "the Metroon and to the Council room to give an

[3] Julian *Discourse* 5, 159a. The fundamental work on the Mother of the gods is P. Borgeaud, *La mère des dieux: de Cybèle à la vierge Marie* (Paris, 1996); most of my knowledge about the Mother and the Metroon derives from Borgeaud's work.

[4] To the great delight of Detienne; see his "Quand les Olympiens prennent l'habit du citoyen," in Sissa and Detienne, *La vie quotidienne des dieux grecs.*

[5] Thompson, "Building on the West Side of the Agora," 205.

account of his public services,"[6] I refuse to believe that the Metroon was mentioned only to help locate the Bouleuterion, whose location, after all, all Athenians knew.

If we add, as some believe, that from the time of Cleisthenes up to the end of the fifth century, one and the same building seems to have been used for the cult of the Mother and for the meetings of the Council, we are compelled to observe that before they formed a closely knit politico-religious complex in the fourth century, there was a time when the sanctuary of the Mother and the ancient Bouleuterion "were one";[7] thus it is hardly surprising that, among second-rank sacrifices, the prytanies could perform sacrifices to the Mother as well as to Peitho (Persuasion), an eminently political deity, or to Apollo (called Patroos insofar as he was considered to be an ancestor of the Athenians).[8]

The Metroon, the Bouleuterion . . . We can certainly pursue this association in one direction or the other—install the temple in the political building, as does the scholiast on Aeschines who sees in the Metroon "a part of the Council room," or make the members of the Boule sit in the Mother's temple: neither solution is devoid of sense, and we would of course very much like to know what was the case "at the beginning." For want of this knowledge, however, we may keep in mind that the association of a divine Mother with civic deliberation is not in the least confined to the city of Athens, since with regard to the Thesmophoria—at which the wives-mothers honor the "Two Goddesses," Mother and Daughter forever linked one to the other—we can observe that "in some cities, the realm of Demeter is largely invested by the political."[9] But whatever the links between the two goddesses postulated by archaeologists—the Mother in the Met-

---

[6] Plutarch *Lycurgus* 31. It is in the Bouleuterion that a magistrate would give an account of his services; the mention of the Metroon has to be explained, since it is not needed in the least here.

[7] See Cerri, "La Madre dei Dei," 155–95, 163, 169–70, 172–73.

[8] Demosthenes *Prooimia* 54 (1460), about 349–346 B.C.

[9] M. Detienne, "Violentes Eugénies," in M. Detienne and J.-P. Vernant, eds., *La cuisine du sacrifice en pays grec* (Paris, 1979), 197, 198 (the Thesmophorion of Thasos), and 199–202.

roon, Demeter in Eleusis—the Mother is not Demeter. Certainly we have encountered the Thesmophoria several times as the very example of the good integration of mothers in the city—to the degree that the Thesmophorion of Thasos, where women mimic men's politics, can without surprise reunite within its walls the most "political" gods—but the idea, however it is formulated, of the Mother giving shelter to the Boule in her temple or of the Council taking in the most savage of divine mothers remains startling.

It is always possible to bypass the difficulty by focusing on the fourth century, when the two buildings, contiguous but not confused, each had their own purpose. But then we notice a new overlap in functions in the Metroon: at that time, besides the cult of the Mother, this structure also contained Athens's public archives.[10] In other words, and to express it in the very words of an Athenian orator, the Mother kept watch[11] over all the written memory of the democracy, or nearly all: laws and decrees (such as the one passed in honor of the men of Phyle who reestablished democracy in the city in 403), indictments in trials (thus, some say, Meletos's *graphē* against Socrates), and accounts and lists of all sorts.[12]

Inviolability, truth, justice: inside the Metroon, the city's archives were under the protection of the sacred. Even if we make allowances for the exaggerations of orators who claim that the erasure of a single law in this place warrants the death penalty or who explicitly prohibit the introduction there of false documents,[13] the question, barely set

---

[10] *Koinà grámmata,* says Demosthenes (*On the False Embassy* 129). See Stella Georgoudi's excellent explanation in "Manières d'archivage," in M. Detienne, ed., *Les savoirs de l'écriture en Grèce ancienne* (Lille, 1988), 221–47.

[11] Dinarchus (*Against Demosthenes* 86) makes her "the guardian" (*phúlax*) of all the laws kept in writing.

[12] Ancient sources are gathered by R. E. Wycherley, *The Athenian Agora,* vol. 3, *Testimonia* (Princeton, 1957), 150–60 (exhaustive dossier of literary and epigraphical evidence). We can assume that texts were also displayed around the Metroon, to judge from a decree dated to the end of the fourth century (*IG* II², 40) concerning the first-fruit offering of wheat consecrated at Eleusis. This decree prescribes its own inscription, in the form of an addition, on the stele formerly raised to record the decree of Chairemonides (end of the fifth century), bearing on the same topic and placed *in front* of the Metroon.

[13] It is true that "to undermine the city's written records is to behave like a traitor,

aside, arises again, intact: how can we account for this vocation of the Mother to protect the written memory of the city?[14]

I would like to offer an answer by way of a close examination of civic representations of a mother's "justice."

As early as Solon we have confirmation that the Mother of the gods could strive for justice: Solon exults in having freed the Athenian land from the stone markers that were once found there, and produces as a witness, "in justice, the very great Mother of the Olympian gods, noble, the black Earth."[15] In another register, a speech of Aeschines suggests in passing that to sit down in desperation by the altar of the Mother is to ask for justice.[16]

But this testimony is not sufficient: we must look to the civic model of the mother, of all mothers, in seeking to understand what earns the Mother the position, at the heart of the political sphere, of "guardian of everything just that has been recorded in writing."

What, then, is a just mother?

Hesiod is first to respond, and we also find an answer implicit in the *Odyssey:* the just mother is a mother who lives under the regime of *díkē*—because, under the government of a good king, the just rulings of justice go together with women giving birth to sons who resemble their fathers.[17] A more elaborate answer is given by Aristotle: much more than an environment propitious to just reproduction, justice, for a woman, is the word used to designate her function

---

a murderer, indeed a sacrilege" ("porter atteinte aux écrits de la cité, c'est se conduire en traître, en meurtrier, voire en sacrilège"), so M. Detienne, "L'espace de la publicité: Ses opérateurs intellectuels," in Detienne and Vernant, *Les savoirs de l'écriture,* 51.

[14] Taking here the opposite view from Thompson, who advances reasons of pure convenience (proximity of the Boule) or contingency ("Building on the West Side of the Agora," 206).

[15] Solon frag. 36 West, lines 3–7. We may perhaps compare the frequent invocation of Earth in oaths with this Earth Mother testifying in court; see also Electra's invocation in Aeschylus *Choephoroi* 148: "by the gods, by Earth and by Justice who brings victory."

[16] *Against Timarchus* 60–61.

[17] On the *Odyssey,* see L. Slatkin, "Genre and Generation in the *Odyssey,*" *Mètis* I (1986): 259–68, especially p. 266; Hesiod *Works and Days* 225–26 and 235.

as a good procreator. "Most of the time," he observes, "daughters tend to resemble their mother, and sons their father"—thus, under the guise of science, the fantasy of the race of women is re-formed, complete in itself. But, the philosopher adds, the opposite can also occur, and it also happens that "children resemble both their parents in parts"—after the fantasy, the reality of a pure coincidence. It still remains to describe the case where norm and nature blend for the happiness of individuals and cities:

> There are also women who give birth to children who always resemble them, and others who have children who resemble their husbands, as happened with a mare from Pharsalia who received the name Just (*dikaía*).[18]
>
> (Aristotle *History of Animals* 586a)

Since legitimate filiation is at the very heart of justice, only the mother who knows what reproduction means deserves the title Just: to reproduce the father means to provide a true replica without any trace remaining on the child of her who nourished and gave birth to him.

(Some advice to the female, and male, denigrators of Freud who accuse him a little too readily of defining woman only by what is lacking. First, read the Greek texts—too numerous to treat here—in which woman is described as a pure receptacle for the father's seed, which she preserves without modifying;[19] then go back over Freud's claims concerning the "stamp of maternal characteristics" in the life of the psyche, especially as regards love, compared with the skull's conformation of the newborn—which "after a protracted labour always bears the form of a cast of the maternal pelvis." Finally, ponder everything that separates—radically—Freudian reflection, about which we can say with good reason that "what is given" is the mothers' part and

---

[18] Aristotle comes back to this example in *Politics* 2.1262a21–24.

[19] The fundamental text on this topic is Aeschylus *Eumenides* 658–61.

"what is earned or won" is the fathers' part,[20] from an understanding of patrilineal extremism, where the father gives everything, and the mother is content to lend the nourishing shelter of her body for a few months.)

No trace of the mother, then. But there is a trace of the father inside the mother's body. Or, more precisely, a trace of the father's inscription. Something similar to writing. Thus King Pelasgus, face to face with the Danaids, who so obviously come from afar with their tanned complexions, puts it in his embarrassment; from supposition to supposition (would they be Lybians, Indians? . . . or maybe Amazons?), an hypothesis arises whose formulation puts an end to our wondering:

> It is the Cyprian [= Aphrodite's] mark that, upon female matrixes,
> has been stamped by male artisans.
>
> (Aeschylus *Suppliant Women* 282–83)

Whether it is engraved on stone or inscribed on currency, the mark is called *kharaktḗr* in Greek; *túpos* is what technical vocabulary designates metaphorically as "matrix": the "mold that after having received an imprint in relief or concave allows the reproduction of it on an object submitted to its action"—metals are stamped thus—or the "original mark of a coin that is engraved intaglio or with a stylus."[21] Drawing out the metaphor of the inscription, the king said *túpos*, but in those *gunaikeîoi túpoi* where male artisans strike their mark, it is *mḗtra*, the Greek name for "matrix," that we must understand behind Pelasgos's words.

And, on the same model, it is with a matrix that we would readily associate—in a way we cannot help but do so—the *Khṓra*, this "third

[20] Excerpts from Freud are taken from "Contributions to the Psychology of Love," *Collected Papers*, trans. Joan Riviere (London, 1949), 4:196; on the Freudian text and the question of the mother's and the father's parts, see M. Moscovici, *Il est arrivé quelque chose. Approches de l'événement psychique* (Paris, 1989), 106–7.

[21] These definitions are based on those in the *Dictionnaire Robert* (s.v. matrix). Let us add completely anachronistically that it is the metaphor of *printing* that best illuminates Aeschylus's text.

kind" of the *Timaeus* "that, however, can offer itself only by shirking all definition, all marks or impressions to which we (say) it was exposed." Not that we must here fix the meaning of *khôra* in the Platonic corpus: such an activity is at the same time necessary and impossible, and we will go along with Jacques Derrida's remarks about the inappropriateness of "quietly speaking," with regard to this passage of the *Timaeus,* "of metaphors, of images, of comparisons."[22] But it is true that reading Pelasgus's words, our impulse—mine at any rate—is to reread Plato's development of *khôra,* this third kind between the perceptible and the intelligible, difficult and indistinct (*amudrós,* like the scarcely legible letters of an archaic inscription in Thucydides), which is receptacle and nurse (*hupodokhê, tithênê*), nature which receives all bodies, impression-carrier for everything, cut into figures by the objects that enter it and imprint themselves (*tupōthénta, ektúpōma*), this element in which (*en hôi*) one is born, and that must be compared, Plato adds, to a mother while the principle must be compared to the father.[23] Because *khôra,* this space so difficult to imagine, in turn illuminates with a bright light the field of representation we had to mark out to try to understand this notion of in between, halfway between perceptible and intelligible: a certain conception of the mother as *en hôi,* and everything following from it, including the fact that "she does not make a couple with the father, in other words, with the paradigmatic model";[24] and perhaps that she simply does not belong to a couple of opposition, which would aptly be a "couple father/son." So that the mother would be "apart," as she has been over this long journey. It is particularly meaningful, nonetheless, that she is understood as such at the very moment when civic

[22] "Qui pourtant ne peut s'offrir qu'en se soustrayant à toute détermination, à toutes les marques ou impressions auxquelles nous la (disons) exposée"; "parler tranquillement"; "de métaphores, d'images, de comparaisons" (J. Derrida, "Chora," in *Poikilia: Études offertes à Jean-Pierre Vernant* [Paris, 1987], especially pp. 267–68 [quotations], 277).

[23] Quotations from *Timaeus* 48e–49a, 50b–d, 51a; *amudrós* in Thucydides 6.54.7.

[24] "Elle ne fait pas couple avec le père, autrement dit avec le modèle paradigmatique" (Derrida). I displace here on the mother Derrida's strong analysis of *khôra* ("Chora," 291).

thought domesticates her as matrix. Apollo Patroos, in the *Eumenides,* does not say otherwise, when he claims she does not deserve the name of birthgiver because she is a simple nurse for the seed planted in her, which she preserves "as a stranger for a stranger."

Even when the city of the fathers annexes the inside of her body as matter to imprint in depth, the mother stays apart. As a result, the presence of the mother in the Agora is perhaps less surprising, provided that one goes in the opposite direction, from the *nósphi* toward civic anchoring: the Mother can well be fond of the mountains and thickets of wilderness; the political space integrates this "elsewhere" and fastens it securely in the Athenian ground, to keep watch over the city's writings.

But it is not yet time to go back to the Mother with a capital letter, for we are not finished with the generic mother, or with the inscription inside her matrix. The inscription, or rather, as I said, the writing. Because—whether imprint, inscription, or mark—it is always suggestively a matter of *grámmata* (of letters and thus of writings). Not that, "voice of an absent person, dwelling house," writing is "a substitute for the mother's womb, the first lodging," as Freud puts it.[25] Fantasized by a Greek, the mother is marked but does not mark, and writing would sooner be the symbolic element of reproduction, because if the woman's inside is like virgin wax, Artemidorus will say the imprints of letters are the children that she receives. Here, then, is the female body, with this sex in the shape of a *délta* that makes itself writing tablet (*déltos*) for the use of men.[26] And when, in the *Oedipus Rex,* the chorus, overwhelmed by the pain of incest, asks Oedipus how the "paternal furrows" (*patrôioi álokes*) in Jocasta's body could endure him,[27] we need to understand that the father's writing on the mother's inside can never be erased.

[25] Freud, *Civilization and Its Discontents,* 38, with Moscovici's commentary (*Il est arrivé quelque chose,* 70–71).

[26] Artemidorus *Oneirocritica* 2.45. The theme is ancient and goes back at least to Sappho: see J. Svenbro, *Phrasikleia: An Anthropology of Reading in Ancient Greece* (Ithaca, 1993), 158–59. Writing tablet: P. DuBois, *Sowing the Body: Psychoanalysis and Ancient Representations of Women* (Chicago, 1988), 28 and 130–66.

[27] *Oedipus Rex* 1211–12; see N. Loraux, "L'empreinte de Jocaste," *L'écrit du temps*

Doubtless we have already moved on to another metaphorical field, and by stringing the metaphors together, we can illuminate one with the other, the plowing with the writing, and the writing by the plowing, through which legitimate reproduction expresses itself officially in the Athenian practice of marriage. We shall evoke then the codified formula of weddings, in which the giving of the woman has for its purpose "the plowing of legitimate children"; certainly the connections between the letter inscribed on a tablet and the furrow plowed in the ground are numerous.[28] But such a move, traditional to be sure, would lead us toward Demeter, all-powerful over furrows, and it is the Mother with whom we are occupied here, in all her specificity.

It is high time to check the associative impulse and go back to the Metroon in the Athenian agora. Because now we can suggest how to explain the presence of archives in the temple of the Mother. We certainly tried to add to the file of the just mother the Solonian fragment about the testimony of the Mother of the gods, assimilated to the black Earth, before the tribunal of time;[29] but this text illuminates only very indirectly the placing of public writings inside the temple of the Mother. It appears now that in dwelling on the paternal inscription inside the matrix of women, we were not only indulging in the pleasures of a detour. If the paternal inscription is necessarily an indelible memory in a mother, housing public writings in the Metroon is the same thing as putting them, if not out of reach of all erasing—Alcibiades, as tradition would have it, did not hesitate to

---

12 (1986): 50–52. Thus we may understand the unmatched gravity of incest with the mother for a Greek, because, in the mother, it is still the father who is encountered, indelibly engraved.

[28] Wedding formula: Menander *Dyskolos* 842–43; furrow metaphor in the tragedians: DuBois, *Sowing the Body,* especially pp. 75–81. See also *Timaeus* 91d: sowing invisible living beings in the matrix, as in a furrow.

[29] Obsessed with the association Earth/woman, Page DuBois concludes a little too quickly that the markers in the ground taken out by Solon have a phallic connotation (*Sowing the Body,* 61–63); we must first give what is hardly an image its explicit sense: the ground was enslaved, now it is free, and the markers should be understood rather as "stigmata" (the mark of the slave).

enter the Metroon to erase the name of a condemned man who had won his favor—at any rate under the protection of a religious ban on adulteration of any kind.

Should we then assume that for civic archives the Metroon is like a mother's body standing ready for the father's writing?[30] In formulating this hypothesis, I want to emphasize the word *like,* for I do not want to metaphorize what the Athenians, as keen as they were on metaphorical thought, did not judge worthy of further explanation (leaving the task to each citizen, if he should so desire, of understanding what is meant).

The essential point remains: accepted into the city, the Mother of the black wrath watches over political imprints just as a mother is supposed to keep paternal marks inscribed deep inside herself. Just as Demeter, as a divine mother, looks after the fecundity of the plowed fields while the fecund furrows of reproduction are inscribed inside human mothers.

Thus the political intends to domesticate feminine excess, which is advantageously converted into a figure of justice. Whether the operation is actually successful is another story. Thus the Erinyes, installed at the foot of the Acropolis under the name of Furies, these black dispensers of justice whom we now call—O *wishful thinking!*—the Kindly Ones, are supposed to protect the city against the very principle they incarnate; but let there be a citizen's blood shed by citizens, and the Avengers will rage again: such is the lesson of the ending of the *Eumenides,* where the old goddesses of shed blood confront Apollo, this son of a father. Similarly, by integrating the Mother in the civic space, did they intend to cast out completely the threat, so often fantasized, of another justice—terrible—by means of which the Mothers' vengeance would threaten fathers? Whatever the answer,

---

[30] Yan Thomas suggests to me that because all institutional systems require a subject, the thinking of a subject demands that we go through a fiction of the body; similarly, in an engraving studied by P. Legendre ("L'institution du corps," in N. Loraux and Y. Thomas, eds., *Le corps du citoyen,* forthcoming), the pope's breast contains all the archives of canon law.

when it comes to human mothers, everyday and domesticated, civilized by marriage and carriers of paternal writings, the citizens seem to have determined that they nevertheless still had enough of a potential for excess in the depths of their grief that they had to enclose their mourning within the narrow limits of regulations.

Too close or too removed. Riveted to the child's body in a childbirth that never ends. Or withdrawn from men's company and unyielding to their prayers. Given over to their *mênis* and raging. Stifling love and murderous hate. Armed, disarmed, there is no doubt that mothers terrify, so that we dress them in black.

Shakespearean mothers: the most beloved, the most hated. Gloucester was certainly well inspired, who, in his initial monologue, attributed only to Nature the wrong that was inflicted on him at birth. Because Richard III says to the Duchess what Gloucester suppressed—the hate of the mother for her son—he instantaneously becomes a victim of this hate, and, from this moment on, he shall not succeed at any of his enterprises. But a Shakespearean son is never able to avoid the very ambivalent confrontation with the one to whom Hamlet declares: "Would it were not so, you are my mother."[31]

I would readily agree to the fiction of a summary typology. There would be some who save the mother, indeed who protect her: thus maybe the Athenians when they install the Mother in the political sphere; and I would perhaps put Freud in the same category, about whose aim I sometimes wonder when he postulates a love so simply simple of a mother for a son,[32] preserving this relationship alone from the ambivalence that weighs on all the others (love of daughters for mother and of mother for daughters, this is another story entirely, not to speak of the bond, essential to psychoanalysis and so problematic, that joins the son to his mother and confronts her with him). There would also be those who make her terrible because they fear her:

---

[31] *Hamlet* 3.4.16.

[32] The answer has to be theoretical; it requires no further reference to Amalia, the young mother so beloved (or so fleetingly that the essential still remains to be imagined).

Shakespeare belongs perhaps to their number, he who lets sons "twist the heart" of their mothers, and purges mythological paradigms of the mother of all maternal reference—in the speech of the comedian declaiming before Hamlet as in the eyes of desperate Lucretia, the grief of Hecuba is only that a wife,[33] and we know that, in the nightingale's song, Philomela has replaced Procne, the killer of her own son.

But the last word belongs to the Greek poet. To the cry of Hecuba over Hector who falls. To Niobe, who, weary of crying, became hungry and nevertheless forever weeps in the mountains and recooks her grief. To the Mother, distraught with mourning and suddenly laughing to the shrill sound of Phrygian music. And we are not afraid anymore, because, whatever we say about them, the terrible Mothers of the Greeks are terribly mothers.

[33] Hecuba: *Hamlet* 2.2.502–18; *The Rape of Lucrece* 1447–55. Philomela: *The Rape of Lucrece,* 1079–82 and 1128–30 (see chap. 6, note 2 above). This shift of signifier may not in this period be the work of Shakespeare alone; besides, in his works, it is in character in each context. The important fact seems to me to be the shift of signifier.

Of Amnesty and Its Opposite

Of Amnesty and Its Opposite

Under the heading "Uses of Oblivion," I would like to talk about amnesty.

But already the step has been taken that, from a purged memory, ends in oblivion. So strongly does the sequence impose itself—amnesty, amnesia—seductive like an etymology, evident like an assonance, necessary it seems (or so we think, at any rate, when we mistrust both oblivion and amnesty on principle). Oblivion, however, could come too quickly or be excessive, when by oblivion we mean the shadow cast by the political on memory. Can we truly see something like a strategy of oblivion in amnesty, the institutional obliteration of those chapters of civic history that the city fears time itself is powerless to transform into past events? It would be necessary for us to be able to forget on command. But in itself, this utterance has little meaning.

There are other ambivalences, too. If oblivion is not an irremediable absence, but, as in the Freudian hypothesis, a presence absent only from itself, a veiled surface sheltering what would only have been repressed, then the aim of amnesty would definitely be paradoxical. Moreover, to take the word literally, what does an amnesty want, what is its proclaimed intention? An erasing from which there is no coming back and no trace? The crudely healed scar of an amputation hence forever memorable, provided that its object be irremediably lost? Or the planning of a time for mourning and the (re)construction of history?

We must arrive at some answer, but I shall abstain from providing any for now and suggest a detour, a way of taking a step back. What about amnesty as it was considered in ancient times, when what we call by that name did not have a name (although the word *amnēstía* was available to this end) but was an utterance that was syntactically doubly restraining? We might as well say that the detour will be Greek, more precisely Athenian, and that the double utterance adjoins a prescription (*ban on recalling misfortunes*) to the taking of an oath (*I shall not recall misfortunes*).

Ban on recalling, I shall not recall. Twice, it is a question of memory in Athens. A rejected memory, but still a memory. Shall we lose sight of oblivion? This is the detour for now. Just long enough to put into perspective what we mean by this word, and better to build up the Greek notion: more threatening, more archaic, and as if original insofar as it hides in the shelter of its opposite, this notion will appear only under negation (but in a very different manner than memory does in Athens). This guarantees a slow decoding at the heart of banned utterances, utterances that are hidden under the reference to memory by a very Greek procedure.

A ban, what is banned. Evidently, the dissonance between the two categories is essential, and it would be better not to be reductive about it.

Two Bans on Memory in Athens

Two bans on recalling in Athens of the fifth century B.C. One at the very beginning of the century, and the other at the very end.

Herodotus makes himself the historian of the first one. Recounting the Ionian revolt in 494, and how the Persians subdued the rebels by capturing Miletus, which they then emptied of people and whose sanctuaries they burned, Herodotus lingers on the reaction to this event of two different peoples of the Ionian family. Formerly deprived of their fatherland—over which event the Milesians had mourned considerably, as befits parents or guests—the inhabitants of Sybaris did not repay the Milesians in kind. On the other hand, the Athenians showed an extreme, not to say excessive, affliction. And more specifically, it happened that

> Phrynichus, having produced a play, the *Capture of Miletus*, the whole theater broke into tears, and he was fined a thousand drachmae for having reminded them of their own misfortunes (*hōs anamnēsanta oikēia kaká*), and they ordered that no one (*mēkéti mēdéna*) should ever make use of this play.
>
> (Herodotus 6.21)

Doubtless, with this very official decree of the Assembly of the people, the Athenians thought they were only forbidding any future representation of the *Capture of Miletus*, sinking Phrynichus's tragedy irresistibly into oblivion. But we will readily ascribe an entirely different significance to this decision, eminently paradigmatic of the Athenian status of civic memory, and the Athenian definition of the tragic. Heavily fined and banned from the stage for having introduced in Athenian theater an action (*drâma*) that is nothing but suffering (*páthos*)[1] for the Athenians, and a family matter—the Ionian family, this family that is also the city, that is in one word the civic identity, this collective self that defines itself by the sphere of what is one's own (*oikeîon*)[2]—by making them recall "their own misfortunes," the first of the great tragedians awakens his fellow citizens—for what I like to consider the first time—to the dangers of recalling, when the object of memory is a source of mourning for the civic self.

---

[1] I take *páthos* 'suffering' from the form *pathoûsi* describing the Milesians (Herodotus 6.21).

[2] On Herodotus's account, see S. Mazzarino's remarks (who translates *oikēia* as "own" in *Il pensiero storico classico*, 2d ed. [Bari, 1983], 1: 107–8). On *oikeîos*, see N. Loraux, "*Oikeios polemos*: La guerra nella famiglia," *Studi storici* 28 (1987): 5–35, as well as "La main d'Antigone," *Mètis* 1 (1986): 165–96.

A long history begins, that of the Athenian practice of memory, and that, also, of tragedy, which we imagine forever marked by this initial check. The Athenian people make it known that they will not bear to see anything on stage that affects them painfully; the tragedians learn the lesson and know how to avoid too current events, unless those events are a source of mourning for others, a mourning tirelessly transformed in a hymn to Athens's glory, as in the *Persians*.[3] A choice as important as that of fiction[4]—or, let us say, *mûthos*—for the tragic genre may perhaps be ascribed to this mandatory departure from current events. At any rate, we should observe that when the *mûthos* takes place in Athens, the tragedy will characteristically be endowed, as in Euripides' Athenian plays, with a "positive" ending; consequently the "real" tragedies, in which the *dráma* is at the same time *páthos,* will take place outside of the city. In the fourth century, Isocrates delights in formulating the law that requires that Athens represent in its own theater crimes originally attached to "other cities."[5]

Thus, at the beginning of the fifth century, Athens commits itself to a well-monitored practice of civic memory.

The second ban, at the very end of the century, aims at preventing any recall of the "misfortunes" that have befallen the very self of the city, torn at its core by civil war. After the military defeat of Athens and the bloody oligarchy of the Thirty, this is the ban on "recalling the misfortunes" that seals the democratic reconciliation in 403. We call this

---

[3] Aeschylus *Persians* 284–85, 287, 824 (as well as Herodotus 5.105). With S. Mazzarino (*Il pensiero storico classico*, 1:107–8), we should note that the Darius of the *Persians* evidently does not recall the victory he won at Ephesus over the Athenians and Ionians.

[4] This is J.-P. Vernant's reading in "Le sujet tragique: Historicité et transhistoricité," in J.-P. Vernant and P. Vidal-Naquet, *Mythe et tragédie* (Paris, 1986), 2: 86–87.

[5] Isocrates *Panathenaicus* 121–23. Athenian tragedies: even taking ambiguity into account, this is the case in Euripides (*Ion, Suppliant Women, Heracleidae*) as well as in Aeschylus's *Eumenides*. As Renate Schlesier brings to my notice, it is undeniable that Athens itself can nevertheless be brought into question; but it is always in an indirect manner, for example, through the opposition Greeks/barbarians in the tragedies of Euripides' Trojan cycle.

an amnesty—modern historians of Greece even make this episode the model amnesty, the paradigm of all those that occidental history will come to know, and already Plutarch uses this term when, conscious of the deep affinity between the two gestures, he associates the "decree of amnesty" (*tò psêphisma tò tês amnēstías*) with the fine imposed on Phrynichus.[6]

The year 403 before our era: hunted down only the day before, having now come back victorious to Athens, the democrats proclaim a general reconciliation with a decree and an oath. The decree proclaims the ban: *mề mnēsikakeîn,* "It is forbidden to recall the misfortunes"; the oath binds all the Athenians, democrats, oligarchs, important people, and "quiet" people who stayed in the city during the dictatorship, but it binds them one by one: *ou mnēsikakḗsō,* "I shall not recall the misfortunes."

Recall the misfortunes, what does this phrase mean—which the compound verb *mnēsikakeîn* expresses formulaically in Athens and in other cities? Once we accept that, under the designation *kaká* 'misfortunes', the Greeks mean what we would more readily call, in a euphemistic mode, events—the disorder in the city—we should pay attention to *mnēsi-,* a form developed from the Greek root for "memory." To judge by the uses of *mnēsikakeîn,* it is less a matter of bringing back to memory, as when Phrynichus provoked an *anámnēsis* (*anmnḗsanta*) among the Athenians, than of recalling *against.* Since *anamnesis* acts upon the citizens of Athens, the verb requires a double object in the accusative—the content of the recollection, and the subject who is reminded; on the other hand, governing in many contexts a dative of hostility, *mnēsikakeîn* suggests that one brandishes a memory in an offensive manner, that one attacks, or that one punishes someone else; in short, that one seeks revenge. Thus, originally neutral, as it was (we suppose) before Phrynichus, the recall of misfortunes becomes a vindictive act at the beginning of the fourth century.

---

[6] *Precepts of Statecraft* 814b–c. We should note that this text, devoted to what it is necessary to recall from the past in order to offer it to the imagination, explicitly retains as objects of memory only acts resulting in oblivion.

Mnēsikakeín: in Plato, the word is used of the victorious party that retaliates with banishing and killing.[7] In Athens after 403, it more specifically designates, in Aristotle as well as in judicial speeches, the act—which is at the same time considered both explicable and illegitimate, and the responsibility for which is regularly that of the democrats—of starting proceedings for acts of civil war.[8]

Mè mnēsikakeín: this is a way of proclaiming that there is a time limit for seditious acts. The aim is to restore a continuity that nothing breaks, as if nothing had happened. The continuity of the city, symbolized by the *aeí* (always: that is to say, each time) of the rotation of duties that is untouched by the conflict between democracy and oligarchy: the magistrate Rhinon, for example, who enters office under the oligarchy and who gives an account of his services in front of the democratic assembly without the least difficulty, is a symbol of this continuity.[9] We also know that the clause excluding the Thirty from the amnesty was voided for those of them who thought themselves faultless enough to be exposed to the people's eyes. But, at the same time and without worrying about contradiction, there is also the continuity of the democracy of the fifth century with the democracy established after the reconciliation, a continuity certainly more difficult to imagine, short of treating the open wound of the dictatorship as a parenthesis; it was enough, then, to purge this oligarchic parenthesis, if not of the "tyranny" (carefully maintained, on the contrary, as an anomaly, acting as a foil for all rhetorical indignation), then at least of the civil war in its reality. Whether the operation was useful is another matter: to judge by all the things that set the "restored," though toned-down, democracy after 403 against the democracy ending in 405, one could wager that no operation of mem-

---

[7] Letter VII, 336e–337a; I follow Luc Brisson's translation (Plato, *Lettres* [Paris, 1987]), who explains the construction of the sentence by grouping *kratésantes mákhais.*

[8] See, for example, Aristotle *Athenian Constitution* 40.2; Isocrates *Against Callimachus* 23 (and 2, where *dikázesthai parà toùs hórkous* is the strict equivalent of *mnēsikakeín*); Lysias *Against Nicomachus* 9; and Andocides *On the Mysteries* 104. Illegitimacy: the act of inadmissibility evoked in *Against Callimachus* 2 attempts to prevent the very existence of such trials, and as Yan Thomas brings to my attention, as with the current prejudicial question, it locks the entire Athenian system against memory.

[9] Aristotle *Athenian Constitution* 38.4.

ory was successful in closing the wound, so deep was the gash made in the city by the conflict.

It is precisely this conflict (of division) that should be expurgated from the history of Athens, in every recollection of the past, by "letting go of events that came before." They subtract them, or rather— this is less obvious—they erase, and it is from this erasing, repeated every time, that they anticipate the benefits of forgetfulness.[10]

Further explanation is needed here: in speaking of erasing, I do not mean to turn to a worn metaphor dear to our modern idiom; I mean to speak Greek, in this case Athenian. In Greek discourse about writing as the preferred tool of politics, the act of erasing (*exaleíphein*) is first a gesture at the same time institutional and very material. Nothing is more official than an erasing; they erase a name from a list (the Thirty hardly had any hesitations), they erase a decree, a law henceforth obsolete (to ban the deeds of the *stásis* from memory, the restored democracy more than once made use of this practice): thus subtraction responds to subtraction. But we should also note that, up to this point, there is nothing in the erasing but the very concrete. To erase is to destroy by additional covering: they coat the surface of a whitewashed official tablet anew, and, once the lines condemned to disappear are covered up, there is a space ready for a new text; similarly, they insert a correction with paint and brush on an inscribed stone, hiding the old letter with a new one. Erasing? Nothing but banal, run-of-the-mill political life. It is not that, here and there, *exaleíphein* is not metaphorical. Then the image of an inner writing appears, drawn in memory or in the mind, and thus susceptible, like all inscriptions, to erasing, whether this erasing is beneficial, when thought, as it develops, gets rids of mistaken beliefs, or whether it is harmful, when it is a matter of doing without mourning. The reconciliation of 403 is distinctive in that political memory is expressed in a register at the same time symbolical and material—not only one, not only the other, and both simultaneously. Erasing plays a double game

---

[10] Andocides *On the Mysteries* 81. Some democratic orators actually speak of forgetfulness, but as of a mistake: see Lysias *Against Eratosthenes* 85 ("They think you are quite forgetful"); see also *Against a Charge of Subverting the Democracy* 2.

then: some decrees are actually erased, but when Aristotle claims that the Athenians behaved well by "erasing the charges (*tàs aitías* 'the reasons [for a trial]') bearing on the earlier period," this erasing, entirely preventive, has no other goal than to ban *mnēsikakeîn*, no other aim than to avoid trials to come, no other effect than that of a speech act, like an oath. Thus it appears that the Athenians set up a close relation of equivalence between a prohibition of memory and erasing.[11]

Let us take one further step forward: few sources verify that there were, on the other hand, democrats who wished to erase—symbolically and perhaps institutionally—the agreements between citizens from both sides, because democrats who dared express themselves in this way were rare.[12] But there were some to be sure who wished "to recall the misfortunes," or more precisely—on this point, Aristotle is explicit—there was at least one, among those who came "back," who started to *mnēsikakeîn;* so the moderate Archinos, having also come back to Athens with the *dêmos* and having thus taken on an aura of prestige, drags this man before the Council and has him put to death without judgment. Whether the story of this unknown democrat, doomed to anonymity because he demonstrated an untimely taste for memory, is historic or serves as an *aítion* for the law of the same Archinos regulating the modalities of the charge after 403, the lesson is clear: the moderate politician is an example (*parádeigma*), and once this promoter of memory was put to death, "no one afterwards recalled the misfortunes."[13] An expiatory victim has been sacrificed to memory; henceforth a fine will be enough to dissuade.

If at least one execution was necessary, it is because, underlying the whole process, there was much at stake for politics: it was a matter of reestablishing the exchange—the Athenians spoke of "the reconcilia-

---

[11] Mistaken beliefs: Plato *Theaetetus* 187b; doing without mourning: Euripides *Hecuba* 590; decrees actually erased: Andocides *On the Mysteries* 76; erasing the charges: Aristotle *Athenian Constitution* 40.3. For the association of the two gestures—prohibition of memory and erasing—see Andocides *On the Mysteries* 79.

[12] Only Isocrates *Against Callimachus* 26: "You were angry at those who said that it was necessary to erase (*exaleíphein*) the agreements."

[13] See Isocrates *Against Callimachus* 2–3. *Aítion:* the unfortunate democrat probably "was the first (*êrxato*)" to *mnēsikakeîn,* rather than "began to" (G. Mathieu, *Discours* [Paris, 1962]). "No one afterwards": Aristotle *Athenian Constitution* 40.2.

tion" (*diallagê*) or "the concord" (*homónoia*)—between citizens who, a few months beforehand, confronted each other, army against army. To this end, it mattered to exonerate those who did not conquer, to isolate the guilty: the Thirty, of course, who, as a matter of fact, already occupied this position; designated numerically, just as often the colleges of magistrates in Greece, they are all the more easy to count then, they who are also manifestly promoters of the conflict. One clause of the agreement—modified, we saw, with a restriction that is not negligible—made an exception to the ban on *mnēsikakeîn* for them alone.[14] The responsibility for the bloodshed thus fixed, all the other Athenians are left, destined to become reconciled. Thus they would not have to consider the notion of a henchman (informers in the service of the tyrants are exonerated, if they did not kill with their own hand, and everything goes on as if no one had done it) and could stick with the notion, a reassuring one, of "quiet" citizens. And during the trials there are actually scores of *kósmioi,* supporters of order, who have nothing to blame themselves for. . . . At the conclusion of the process, the city will be reconstituted, one and indivisible from the official praises of Athens.

I spoke of political stakes. Were I an Aristotelian, I would have to say that politics itself was at stake. Witness Aristotle himself concerning Archinos: "He acted as a good politician" (*politeúsasthai kalôs*); and concerning Athenian democrats: "They seem to have used their past misfortunes in the most beautiful and most civic manner (*kállista kaì politikótata*)." But already Isocrates gave the real story: "Since we mutually gave each other pledges . . . , we govern ourselves in a manner as beautiful as collective (*hoútō kalôs kaì koinôs politeuómetha*) as if no misfortune had happened to us."[15] Everything is clear: politics is to act as if everything were fine. As if nothing had happened. Neither conflict nor murder nor ill-feelings (nor resentment).

[14] Some other oligarchic bodies are to be added. see Aristotle *Athenian Constitution* 39.6 and Andocides *On the Mysteries* 90. On the use that citizens accused of antidemocratic intrigues make of it, see Lysias 25.5, 16, 18.

[15] Aristotle *Athenian Constitution* 40.2 and 3 (where we note that the Athenians "use" their misfortunes just as, in Herodotus, they forbid anyone to "use" Phrynichus's tragedy); Isocrates *Against Callimachus* 46.

Of politics, then, which would start where vengeance stops. Thus, in the tradition of Isocrates and Aristotle, Plutarch will praise Poseidon, once pretender to the title of master of Athens, but defeated by Athena, for his lack of resentment (*aménitos*); that is to say, the god was "more political" (*politikóteros*) than Thrasybulus, leader of the democrats who returned to the city and as a result of his victory enjoyed an easy generosity. And the same Plutarch adds that the Athenians recorded this divine clemency doubly: by subtracting the anniversary of the conflict, a grievous memory for the god, from the calendar, and by raising an altar to Lethe, Oblivion, in the Erechtheion.[16] A negative operation—the subtraction—and the establishing of oblivion on the Acropolis (the very place the Athenians like to call the City), in the depths of the temple of Athena Polias: erasing of the conflict, promotion of *léthē* as the basis of life in the city. And Plutarch also gives this as a definition of the political (*politikón*): that it deprives—this is perhaps the fundamental subtraction—hate of its eternal character (*tò aídion*).[17]

These are Athenian matters, to be sure. But how to keep them at a distance up till the end? I have resisted the demon of analogy, who, more than once, whispered to me, not inappropriately, such and such a parallel with France of the Liberation, and the debates that took place from 1945 to 1953 about the legitimacy of the purge, or a comparison with the repressing and forgetting of these events we would like to be certain are actually behind us, since they took place in the France of Vichy.[18] But I cannot refrain, by way of a quasi-contemporary counterpoint, from quoting this conversation of 24 July 1902, reported by Jules Isaac:

> Péguy tells me that tolerance leads to degradation, that it is necessary to hate. I asked him: "But what is hate?" "Nonamnesty."[19]

---

[16] Plutarch *Table Talk* 9.6 (in *Moralia* 741b); *On Brotherly Love* 18 (*Moralia* 489b–c).

[17] Plutarch *Solon* 21.2.

[18] See H. Rousso, "Vichy, le grand fossé," *Vingtième siècle* 5 (1985): 55–79, as well as *Le syndrome de Vichy, 1944–198 . . .* , (Paris, 1987).

[19] "Péguy me dit que la tolérance conduit à l'avilissement, qu'il faut haïr. Je lui ai demandé: "Mais qu'est-ce que la haine?—La non-amnistie," (J. Isaac, *Expériences de*

In 1900, the Dreyfus affair had experienced its first turning point with the vote of amnesty, but in his anger,[20] Péguy was among those who did not want the matter to be closed, because there was no matter to begin with. And it must be added that Péguy, certainly not very "political" in the Greek sense (the lasting sense?) of the word, broke with Jaurès in 1902.

I close the parenthesis but ask the question that comes up again and again, like the most forbidden of temptations: what if the word "political" had more than one meaning? Or, more exactly, appealing to the distinction between politics and the political: could there be a Greek politics that did not base itself on oblivion? Does this politics, which would take into account the inevitability of the conflict, which would allow that the city is by definition doomed to divide itself into two, and not between "tyrants" on one side and Athenians on the other, does this politics, which is at the same time inimical and communal, have any other existence than as a construction of the imagination?[21] It so happens that if the construction is indeed a Greek one, the inimical community seems to have been thus constructed only as the fiction of an origin always already outmoded: in the beginning was the conflict; then came the *pólis* . . . And, endlessly, amnesty would then reinstitute the city against recent misfortunes. Or rather, against the original *mûthos*.

Clearly there is no way out. It is better to take things back toward oblivion and what, in Greece, makes the stakes so high.

To Forget Nonoblivion

Let us decode the strategy of Athenian memory, concentrating on some aspects that are homologous to more generally Greek models. From here on, the discussion is openly about oblivion.

---

ma vie, vol. 1, *Péguy* [Paris, 1963], 282). On the "contemporaneity" of the Dreyfus affair, see M. Winock, "Les affaires Dreyfus," *Vingtième siècle* 5 (1985): 19–37.

[20] See J.-M. Rey, *Colère de Péguy* (Paris, 1987).

[21] See N. Loraux, "Le lien de la division," *Le cahier du Collège international de philosophie* 4 (1987): 102–24.

We begin with the epilogue of the *Odyssey*. At the news of the suitors' murder, there is a great deal of emotion in the city of Ithaca. People gather in the agora, with heavy hearts. Eupeithes, father of Antinoos, who was Odysseus's first target, speaks: *álaston pénthos*, mourning that cannot be forgotten (mourning that does not want to forget), holds him, and he calls for revenge on the murderers. A wise speech is given in response by a wise man, who pleads for the rights of the present. Deaf to the arguments of Eupeithes the "Persuasive," the majority side with this (good) viewpoint; the rest of the people run to their weapons. Against the backdrop of this urgent situation, a dialogue between Zeus and Athena takes place: let the people of Ithaca exchange oaths, and the gods will create oblivion (*éklēsin théōmen*) of the murder.[22] Peace will come back. For now, the fighting begins: Eupeithes falls, as do others still in his company. Then Athena restrains Odysseus's arm (saying to her favorite: "Put an end to the conflict of a too even-sided war"). Solemn oaths are exchanged. End of the *Odyssey*.

As if in echoing response, we have the wish of the politically committed poet Alcaeus, the first to pronounce in his verses the word *stásis*:

> May we forget this anger (*ek dè khólō tôde lathoímetha*).
> Let us free ourselves from the heart-eating rebellion and civil war,
> which one of the Olympians has aroused.
>
> (Alcaeus frag. 70 Campbell)

Eklêthomai in Alcaeus, *éklēsis* in the *Odyssey*: everything starts with a call to oblivion. To forget not only the bad deeds of others but one's own anger so that the bond of life in the city may be renewed. Hence the question: are we to suppose that something like a story intervenes between the archaic wish for oblivion and the Athenian ban on memory? What could have happened between the oblivion that was spoken for and the prescription not to recall? Since once again we must try to construct from history, I suggest that between oblivion of wrath

---

[22] *Odyssey* 24.485.

and the recall of misfortunes we place the poetic notion of "oblivion of ills."

This oblivion of the painful present, which the poet's song celebrating the glory of past men brings, would then be positive when it is conferred by the Muses, daughters of Memory—themselves, however, defined as *lēsmosúnē kakôn* 'oblivion of ills'. The oblivion of a very recent bereavement, even if it is imputed to the instantaneous power of the inspired word, has to be free from all ambiguity.[23] Already in Homer, at any rate, there is doubt about this "beneficial" oblivion, when Helen has recourse to a drug and a story to tear Telemachus and Menelaus away from Odysseus's *álaston pénthos* in book 4 of the *Odyssey*. Antidote to bereavement and wrath, *nēpenthés, ákholon, kakôn epílēthon hapantôn,* the drug dispenses oblivion of all ills. And what ills!

> And whoever drank it when it had been mixed in the wine bowl,
> for that day he would let no tears down his cheeks,
> not if his mother or father died,
> and not if someone killed his brother or his own son in
> front of him with the bronze, and he saw it with his own eyes.
>
> (*Odyssey* 4.222–26)

To weep over father and mother is a duty that allows no exception, and the obligation of avenging the murder of a son or brother is particularly strong.[24] As immediate as its effect is temporary, the drug can indeed substitute for mourning the "charm"—itself eminently ambiguous—"of the tale"[25] and the pleasures of the feast, though for a

---

[23] Positive oblivion: M. Detienne, *Les maîtres de vérité dans la Grèce archaïque* (Paris, 1967), 69–70; oblivion of ills: Hesiod *Theogony* 55; recent bereavement: *Theogony* 98–103.

[24] See especially *Iliad* 9.632–33 (criticizing Achilles, who is walled in by his refusal, Ajax claims that one must accept compensation even from the murderer of a brother or a son, which is a way of suggesting that the desire for vengeance is never as strong as it is in this case), as well as *Odyssey* 24.433–435 (Eupeithes' speech).

[25] This is the title of the study by R. Dupont-Roc and A. Le Boulluec: "Le charme du récit (*Odyssée,* IV, 218–289)," in *Écritures et théorie poétiques. Lectures d'Homère, Eschyle, Platon, Aristote* (Paris, 1976); see also A. Bergren, "Helen's Good Drug,"

time it nonetheless cuts the one who drinks it off from society. Such is the ultimate extreme of oblivion of ills, this *phármakon*—a cure for pain, but a poison for human existence, insofar as it is eminently contractual.

The difference between the durable political ban on pursuing a vengeance that would be hurtful to the community and the charm that dispels mourning every time, though only temporarily, is obvious. By swearing not to recall previous misfortunes, the Athenian citizen affirms that he forgoes vengeance, and, to put himself under the double authority of the city, which issues decrees, and of the gods, who punish, he also asserts the control he will maintain over himself as subject; conversely, sweet oblivion comes from elsewhere, be it a gift of the Muses or of the poet, an effect of Helen's drug or of wine (in many contexts) or of the sheltering motherly breast (in book 22 of the *Iliad*); if it is presented with insistence as the oblivion of what cannot be forgotten, no approval, no consent is required from the one it befalls, who, momentarily subjected to this bracketing of misfortunes, is perhaps deprived of everything that made up his identity.

Because, not to give to oblivion all of its power, what is translated passively as "unforgettable" is also—I propose—what we should call the *unforgetful*:[26] the very thing, in Greek poetics, that does not forget and that inhabits the mourner so that it says "I" in the mourner's voice. This is what must be voided through recourse to the drug of "oblivion of ills"; this is, perhaps, what the Athenians prefer to avert in their own name by a decree and an oath. Despite the obvious parallel between formulas, no word-for-word transposition can transform the political ban on memory into a direct avatar of *léthē kakôn*. Still it is

---

in S. Kresic, ed., *Contemporary Literary Hermeneutics and Interpretation of Classical Texts* (Ottawa, 1981), 200–214.

[26] The "unforgetful" has much in common with the "inflexible thing" ("la chose intraitable") that J.-F. Lyotard considers in "A l'insu," in "Politiques de l'oubli," *Le genre humain* 18 (1988). On *álastos / alástōr* and the uncertainty between "unforgettable" and "unforgetful," see L. Slatkin, "The Wrath of Thetis," *Transactions of the American Philological Association* 116 (1986): 19n.

necessary to deconstruct this phrase in order to identify the unforgettable under the very generic designation of "ills" (of "misfortunes": *kaká*). The command *mè mnēsikakeîn* agrees less with *léthē kakôn* in its menacing sweetness than it is a way, by avoiding any explicit reference to oblivion, of canceling the never-formulated oxymoron that is hidden under "oblivion of ills": the oblivion of nonoblivion.

Let us draw the map of what does not forget and what is not forgotten. I named mourning, and wrath, which Helen's drug dissolves and which Alcaeus's insurgents wish they could forget; similarly, much later, in a small Arcadian city, wrath will replace the misfortunes not to be recalled during a reconciliation (and *mnēsikholân* is substituted for *mnēsikakeîn*).[27] They did not think any differently in the reconciled Athens of the end of the fifth century: because to stick to wrath would be to immortalize as the most precious of goods the past of the conflict that does not want to be past (the misfortunes); conversely, anyone who wants to attack the Thirty must be able with impunity to advise the Athenian jurors to oppose the tyrants with "the same anger as at the time of the exile."[28]

Mourning and wrath: we will perhaps recall "the extreme grief" of the Athenians at the capture of Miletus. It so happens that the verb *huperákhthomai* (with which, in the extreme, Herodotus doubtless means to indicate excess) is a quasi *hapax*, since to the occurrence in Herodotus, we can add only a single use, in Sophocles' *Electra:* the coryphaeus's advice to Electra, overwhelmed by the thought of a forgetful Orestes, is to abandon "a too painful wrath" (*huperalgê khólon*), and to give to those she hates "neither too much affliction nor complete oblivion" (*mếth' . . . huperákhtheo mết' epiláthou*). On one side, oblivion; on the other, living memory that bears no other name than excess of grief. In Sophocles, Electra is in fact the perfect incarnation of this living memory that, hardly metaphorically, is a goad, of this grief-wrath that characterizes Achilles (*khólon thumalgéa*), and when she claims *ou láthei m'orgá*, she says not only "My anger does not

---

[27] Alpheira inscription (third century B.C.): T. Riele, *Mnemosyne* 21 (1968): 343.
[28] Lysias *Against Eratosthenes* 96.

escape me" or "I do not forget my anger," but also "My anger does not forget me." As if only anger gave to the self the courage to be entirely given to anger, because for the subject, anger is uninterrupted presence of self to self.[29]

It is left to the citizen-spectators gathered in the theater to guess what, for the city, is the ultimate danger in this anger that does not forget, because it is the worst enemy of politics: anger as mourning makes the ills it cultivates "grow" assiduously, and it is a bond that tightens itself until it resists all untying.[30] Dread wrath . . . And with reason: in this case, tragedy borrows the notion from the most ancient poetic tradition, and most particularly from epic, which from the first word of the *Iliad* gives to this very active affect the name *mênis*. Wrath of Achilles and, later, wrath of mourning mothers, from Demeter to Clytemnestra. If it were not for Achilles, whose *mênis* is in all Greek memories, I would readily say that we have here a female model of memory,[31] which the cities try to confine within the anti- (or ante-) political sphere. And, in fact, wrath in mourning, the principle of which is eternal repetition, willingly expresses itself with an *aeí*,[32] and the fascination of this tireless "always" threatens to set it up as a powerful rival to the political *aeí* that establishes the memory of institutions.[33]

---

[29] *huperákhthomai:* Herodotus 6.21.1; coryphaeus's advice: Sophocles *Electra* 177–78. For the goad, see Sophocles *Oedipus Rex* 1317–18: "How the sting of the goads has entered me together with the memory of evils (*mnémé kakôn*)." *khólon thumalgéa: Iliad* 9.260, 565; *ou láthei m'orgá: Electra* 222.

[30] *Electra,* 259–60, 140–42, 230, 1246–48; *áluton* in the *Iliad:* the fetters (13.37) and the bond of war (13.360). We will recall that, in civic language, the noun most often used of the reconciliation—including in the year 403—is *diálusis* 'untying' (see Aristotle *Athenian Constitution* 39.1, as well as 38.4 and 40.1), as if civil war were the strongest of bonds.

[31] As regards Achilles, Laura Slatkin, in *The Wrath of Thetis* (Berkeley, 1991), suggests that the hero's *mênis* is a displaced rereading of the "wrath" of his mother, Thetis.

[32] Among Lyotard's categories, it falls under "identical repetition" ("répétition identique"), a mode of sentence in which the mark is upon the speaker and not, as in the "Jewish" sentence, on the addressee (*Le Différend* [Paris, 1983], 157).

[33] *Aeí* of Electra: nineteen instances in Sophocles' *Electra* (we should note that

Two more words on this *mênis*, considered dangerous from the very beginning, to the point that whoever is the seat of it is prohibited from using the very name, to the point that the hypogrammatical utterance of the *Iliad*—*I renounce my *mênis*—is never pronounced.[34] *Mênis*: what lasts, what holds well, and nevertheless is doomed, as if by necessity, to become the object of renunciation. *Mênis*: a word to hide the memory whose name is concealed by it.[35] Another memory, much more formidable than *mnémê*. A memory that reduces itself completely to nonoblivion. In fact, we may guess that, in nonoblivion, the negation must be understood in its performativeness: the "unforgetting" establishes itself. And, just as it was necessary to forget the strength of the denial hidden behind the "ills," a recurrent utterance shows the renunciation of memory-anger: it is necessary to deny—assuming that it is possible—the denial that has stiffened upon itself.

Which takes us back to *álaston pénthos*, this mourning that refuses to accomplish itself.[36]

Álastos, then: like *alếtheia*, it is built on a negation of the root of oblivion. And yet it is a very different way of not being in oblivion. It

---

this *aeí* disappears and does not return until Orestes takes action). *Aeí* and institutional memory: [Lysias] *Against Andocides* 25, where it is the entity Athens (*Athênai*) and not the collectivity of Athenians (*Athênaîoi*) that is the subject all-memory (*aeímnēstoi*). As for the antepolitical aspect of *mênis*, we might doubt that such a thing exists if we consider, with L. Gernet (*Recherches sur le développement de la pensée juridique et morale en Grèce* [Paris, 1917], 148), that the verb *mēníō* designates (always?) a collective feeling in Herodotus.

[34] I am referring here to the remarkable analysis of C. Watkins, "A propos de *mênis*," *Bulletin de la société de linguistique* 72 (1977): 187–209. See now L. Muellner, *The Anger of Achilles: Mênis in Early Greek Epic* (Ithaca, 1996).

[35] Popular etymology relates the word to *ménō*, because it concerns a lasting wrath (Chantraine, *Dictionnaire étymologique de la langue grecque*); in spite of Chantraine, I consider the etymology that makes *mênis* a deformation of an original *mnânis* (Watkins, "A propos de *mênis*," 205–6; Muellner, *Anger of Achilles*, app.) compelling.

[36] See P. Pucci's remarks in *Odysseus Polutropos: Intertextual Readings in the "Odyssey" and the "Iliad"* (Ithaca, 1987), 199.

is hardly surprising that in Greek language and thought, *alḗtheia* has prevailed as the "positive" noun for truth, while prose forgot *álastos*. It is doubtless the result of the same euphemizing process that, in place of the verb *alasteîn*, equivalent of Arcadian *erinúein*, "to be enraged" (where we easily recognize the vengeful Erinys), classical prose substituted the less threatening *mnēsikakeîn*, this "opposite of amnesty."[37]

Mourning, wrath. And the philologists wonder: mourning or wrath? But, in *alasteîn*, this choice once more belongs to the realm of the indeterminable. Which for all that does not mean that the verb functions, without reference to its etymology, as a derivative of *pénthos*, to which, so often, *álaston* is adjoined,[38] or of *khólos*, but rather that mourning and wrath are naturally associated with each other insofar as they both participate in nonoblivion. *Alast-*, then: matrix of meaning to express the *páthos* (or, in Phrynichus's version, the *drâma*) of an irreparable loss, be it a disappearance (*álaston pénthos* of Penelope at the thought of Odysseus, of Tros weeping over his son Ganymede in the *Homeric Hymn to Aphrodite*) or a death (*álaston pénthos* of Eupeithes). And this *páthos* is piercing: *álaston odúromai*, "I grieve without forgetting," says Eumaios to Odysseus.[39] Or rather: Never do I forget to grieve, I cannot stop grieving. Thus it turns out that, just as *mênis*, *álaston* expresses the atemporal duration, immobilized in a negative will, and immortalizing the past in the present.

Insomnia of Menelaus, blood of the parricide and the incest that Oedipus cannot forget: there is an obsessive component to *álaston*, a relentless presence that occupies, in the strong sense of the word, the

---

[37] "Contraire de l'amnistie," so Gernet (*La pensée juridique et morale*, 324–25); Gernet glosses *alastêin* as "to be irritated by a wrath that does not forget" ("être irrité d'un courroux qui n'oublie pas").

[38] Cf. G. Nagy, in the mode of "as if" (*Comparative Studies in Greek and Indic Meter* [Cambridge, Mass., 1974], 258).

[39] The *mênis* of Achilles against Agamemnon doubtless arises from Achilles' loss of *timḗ*, not from the loss of someone dear; but not only does he behave precisely as if he had lost more than a son or a brother, which, while it would still require compensation (*Iliad* 9.632f.), surpasses all *timḗ*, but it will not be long before he knows—because of this very *mênis*—the *álaston pénthos* of having lost his double. *álaston odúromai*: *Odyssey* 14.174.

subject and does not leave. Another example: before the final duel with Achilles, Hector begs his adversary to exchange a reciprocal promise not to mutilate the corpse of the dead enemy. Refusal of Achilles: "Do not, *álaste,* talk of agreements." And he adds that there can no more be a faithful treaty between them than between the wolf and the lamb, before concluding: "You will pay all at once for the sorrows of my companions, whom you killed with the fury of your spear." *Álaste:* "accursed," some translate. And there is something of that: Achilles knows that, as far as he is concerned, Hector is unforgettable, like an obsession, just as Patroclus is. Unforgettable in that he killed the one whom Achilles neither wants to nor can forget.[40]

And here is the murderer side by side with his victim in nonoblivion. Which leads me to call up yet another derivative of the root *alast-: alástōr,* the name of the criminal insofar as he has "committed unforgettable acts (*álēsta*), things that will be remembered for a long time," Plutarch says;[41] but also the name of the avenging demon of the dead victim, who tirelessly pursues the murderer.

Nonoblivion is a ghost. *Alástōr,* or *alitḗrios,* what "wanders," in popular etymology (from the verb *aláomai*), or what must absolutely be avoided, in Plutarch (*aleúasthai*).[42]

Did the Greeks live, as the often-quoted title of a book puts it, "in the grip of the past"?[43] The fascination that becomes manifest at every mention of "unforgetting mourning" would definitely seem to indicate that they did. But we must go the whole way; because they recognized it perhaps and were on their guard, as with many of their fascinations, the Greeks have not ceased (and this since the *Iliad* and Achilles' wrath, however superbly dramatized) to try to cast out nonoblivion as the most threatening of the forces of insomnia.[44] Ideally, as

---

[40] Insomnia of Menelaus: *Odyssey* 4.108; Oedipus: Sophocles *Oedipus at Colonus* 1672; refusal of Achilles: *Iliad* 22.261.

[41] Plutarch *Greek Questions* 25, in *Moralia* 297a.

[42] Ibid.

[43] B. A. Van Groningen, *In the Grip of the Past: Essay on an Aspect of Greek Thought* (Leiden, 1953).

[44] I think here of Y. Yerushalmi, *Zakhor: Histoire juive et mémoire juive,* trans.

at the end of the *Oresteia*, it should be neutralized without being completely lost: it should be domesticated by being installed in the city, defused, indeed turned against itself. Thus, by the will of Athena, the Erinyes proclaim that they renounce their fury and agree to keep watch at the foot of the Areopagus while the city sleeps.[45] But this is a delicate operation, such as only a divinity can bring to a successful conclusion. And when wrath reclaims its autonomy and *stásis al-itēriódēs* comes in turn,[46] everything must be done to avert the threat of *álaston:* then, not being able really to forget it, they will forget it in words, in order to forbid memory of misfortunes.

Everything happened between negations: since the privative *a-* of *álaston* will always be more powerful than any verb "to forget," we might as well avoid *alasteín* and have recourse to *mnēsikakeín,* even if it means bringing this memory definitively under negation. All this under the protection of the most inflexible of negations: *mḗ,* which in itself expresses the ban.

Power of the Negative, Strength of the Negation

Nonoblivion is all-powerful insofar as it has no limits—and especially not those of a subject's interiority.

Let us go back to Hector *álastos.* Or, to have recourse to a more common term, to *alástōr.* Between the killer and the vengeful demon of the dead victim, nonoblivion is undivided only because it surpasses both; it is between them, but also very much before and very much after, and they themselves are absorbed in it. Thus Plutarch can now make *alástōr* the designation of the criminal and treat this word under the heading "anger of demons" (*mēnímata daimónōn*) and speak of

---

E. Vigne (Paris, 1984), 118–19, quoting Borges and Nietzsche (*Considérations in-actuelles,* trans. G. Bianquis [Paris, 1964], 119) on what threatens contemporary histo-riography.

[45] Aeschylus *Eumenides* 690–93, 700–706.

[46] See Plato *Republic* 5.470d6; *alitérios,* from which *alitēriódēs* is derived. Although it has a different etymology, the formal proximity to *alástōr* nevertheless makes it a doublet of that word (Chantraine, *Dictionnaire,* s.v. *aleítēs*).

those spirits that we call unforgetting avengers (*alástores*) and blood-avengers (*palamnaîoi*), as they pursue the memory of ancient (*palaiá*), foul, and unforgettable (*álēsta*) acts.

(Plutarch *Obsolescence of Oracles* 418b–c)

In one case as in the other, he uses the unforgettable as an explanatory principle. That being the case, it is certainly vain to build a history of the word, as philologists might, where *alástōr* would be, for example, first the avenger, then the killer; but it is not enough either to invoke a "law of participation," if we are then to stick with the notion of a "point of departure" that can be indifferently the defiled guilty one or the "ghost."[47] Unless we would ascribe to this ghost the model of the principle of nonoblivion: much more than "the polluting act"[48] but also much more than a simple inner state. At the same time outside and inside, sinister reality and psychic experience, as L. Gernet very well expressed it with regard to the Erinys. With the exception that in this case he speaks of "supernatural . . . reality," and that, concerning nonoblivion, I would prefer to insist on its *materiality*, indissociable from its psychic dimension.

Let a chorus of the *Electra* be where, to multiply the negations still further, the affirmation of nonoblivion gives way to the declaration of nonamnesty:

He never forgets (*oú pot' amnasteî*), your begetter, the leader of the Greeks,
and neither does the ancient brazen axe with double edge
that killed him in shameful outrage.

(Sophocles *Electra* 481–85)

Neither the dead victim—who, in the *Choephoroi*, was asked to recall the fatal bath—nor the murder instrument, also believed to be un-

---

[47] History: Chantraine, *Dictionnaire*, s.v. *alástōr;* "law of participation": Gernet, *La pensée juridique et morale*, 319–20.

[48] Of which R. Parker, *Miasma: Pollution and Purification in Early Greek Religion* (Oxford, 1983), 108–9, would like to make the unifying principle, because it centers everything on pollution.

forgetting: the dyad of the victim and of the death weapon is apparently asymmetrically substituted for the couple of the deceased and the murderer.[49] Encompassing time and space completely, nonoblivion is everywhere, active at every stage of the process. It is there for the materiality of the *álaston* that silently keeps watch against oblivion. Still this list would be incomplete if we did not add to it the "misfortune" (*kakón*) itself, equally credited with refusing amnesty (but we know that "the misfortunes" euphemistically replace the "unforgetting" in compound verbs).[50] Again, a few verses of the *Electra* bear witness:

> Never to be veiled, . . . never to be undone (*oú pote katalúsimon*),
> never to forget (*oudé pote lēsómenon*), so great
> is our sorrow.

> (1246–47)

"Never will sorrow forget":[51] it is Electra who is speaking, yet no Greek hero believes in his own inner autonomy more than Electra. As if the undivided[52] and silent force in the subject became pure will intent on its staying power: control, perhaps, but who is controlling whom in this matter?

Electra, of course, believes she is; at any rate, she lets what wants to

[49] Aeschylus *Choephoroi* 491–93. We will note that the murder weapon is no longer a tool, but a subject credited with the killing of Agamemnon; thus in the Prytaneum, Athenian law judges objects that have "caused" the death of a man; see M. Simondon, *La mémoire et l'oubli dans la pensée grecque* (Paris, 1982), 218–19.

[50] We may add to this list the evocation of Phineus's sons, blinded by a stepmother and the orb of whose eyes is itself labeled *alástōr* in the *Antigone* (974).

[51] Mazon (Collection des universités de France) retreats before the evidence and resorts to the passive voice; Simondon (ibid.) chooses a "voluntarily equivocal" ("volontairement équivoque") translation: "who cannot know oblivion" ("qui ne peut pas connaître l'oubli"); with Jebb, the illustrious English editor of Sophocles, we must understand "one sorrow which cannot forget."

[52] Perhaps something of this undividedness can still be seen in the double accusative—of the person recalling and of the object recalled—governed by *anamimnéskō* (the verb that designates Phrynichus's intervention in Herodotus).

speak inside herself speak repetitively. And, as if one never asserted something better than in denying it, she uses only negative utterances:

> In the midst of dreadful things, I shall not
> hold on to these calamities.
>
> (223–24)

or again:

> For this will be called indissoluble (*áluta keklḗsetai*),
> and I shall never cease from my troubles.
>
> (230–31)

A negation, a verbal form in the future. Refusal and control of time, such appears to be the preferred linguistic formula to assert the oblivionless existence of Electra. But there is also the recourse to negations in series, accumulations in which logic that deducts and cancels threatens to lose itself to the profit of an assertion with a purely negative intensity:

> But I shall not cease from my lament and
> my wretched cries.
>
> . . . .
>
> And I shall not cease, like a nightingale,[53] killer of her young,
> with a loud cry, in front of my father's doors,
> to make it echo for all.
>
> (103–10)

Here is one sentence, only one, where no grammarian could find his bearings; let us wager that the Athenian public understood in it the intensity of the refusal. Electra also says:

[53] See N. Loraux, "Le deuil du rossignol," in *Varia* 7 of *Nouvelle revue de psychanalyse* 34 (1986): 251–76.

> I do not wish to abandon this,
> and not to lament my wretched father.

$$(131-32)$$

And the negative formulation becomes a claim for omnipotence and a plan for eternity. Nothing of that recourse to litotes we sometimes think is detectable in the utterance of nonoblivion.[54] Just the opposite, the reduplication that reinforces the negation, as in *oú pote amnasteî* 'No, he does not forget,' or the eternity of a future perfect (*táde áluta keklếsetai* 'Forever it will be called indissoluble').[55] It is up to us, listening to Freud, to understand in all these utterances the same denial, and the confession, made without the speaker's knowledge, that in fact one shall renounce and disown the wrath to which the future gave assurances of an unlimited becoming; it is up to us especially to understand the confession that the excessive negation will nevertheless be fought—vanquished, or at least silenced, and already forgotten—by another negation, for renunciation also expresses itself with a great many verbs meaning "to deny": *apeîpon* in the case of Achilles, and *apennépō* in the case of the Erinyes, compelled to revoke the prohibitions they had uttered against Athens.[56]

Because the Unforgetful has always been the Forgotten.[57]

To put an end to the game of the double negation, it is time to go back to Athens of 403, to that decree and to that oath that proclaim amnesty.

Expressed in an indirect style, as decrees must be, in which writing at the same time presents and subordinates to itself the statement that is effectively expressed,[58] the prohibition of memory is ready to inte-

---

[54] Watkins, "A propos de *mênis*," 209, commenting on the formula *ou . . . lélēthe* (Solon 13 West, line 25).

[55] See C. J. Ruijgh, "L'emploi onomastique de *keklêsthai*," in *Mélanges Kamerbeek* (Amsterdam, 1976), 379.

[56] *Iliad* 19.67, 35, 74–75; Aeschylus *Eumenides* 957.

[57] "L'Oublié": J.-F. Lyotard, *Heidegger et "les juifs"* (Paris, 1988).

[58] In comedy, on the other hand, the prohibition is often uttered in a direct style

grate itself—as a citation—in a historian's narrative or in those paradigmatic recollections of the past that the orators use ("Then the 'prohibition against recalling the misfortunes' came under an oath": *tò mè mnēsikakeîn*). The prohibition has been transformed into a *rhêma*, a reified saying, turning into a maxim, into a definitely noncurrent exemplum.[59] Because "the narrative is perhaps the genre of discourse in which the heterogeneity of genres of sentences and even that of genres of discourses find the best place to make themselves forgotten."[60]

The city forbids, then, taking the stance of eternity, but it masks the formulation of this act of forbidding. The oath is left, which must be taken by all the citizens, but one by one. Or again, by each individual Athenian, uttering in the first person: "I shall not recall the misfortunes." *Ou mnēsikakêsō:* as regards the ban, which is always subordinate to the reminder that there was a decision, the oath is a speech act.[61] It decrees, by engaging the oath taker, but the subject gains by speaking as an "I," and by endowing his commitment with the power of future negative utterances. I shall not recall: I shall prevent myself from recalling. Thus each citizen makes sure at the same time of himself and of the future.

Yet everything can be turned upside down once more. To silence memory, the Athenian oath taker certainly speaks in the same mode as Electra proclaiming her will not to forget. It is not, however, an

---

(Aristophanes *Lysistrata* 590; *Ploutos* 1146); but, spoken to a single addressee, it becomes burlesque.

[59] Historians' narrative: Xenophon *Hellenica* 2.4.43; Aristotle *Athenian Constitution* 39.6 (cites the text of the agreement); see also Andocides *On the Mysteries* 77, 79, 81, as well as Thucydides 4.74; citation of orators: Aeschines *On the Embassy* 176; *rhêma*: Aeschines *Against Ctesiphon* 208.

[60] "Le récit est peut-être le genre de discours dans lequel l'hétérogénéité des genres de phrases et même celle des genres de discours trouvent au mieux à se faire oublier" (Lyotard, *Le Différend*, 218; on the noncurrency of the citation, see p. 55).

[61] Quoted as such, the oath breaks off a narrative for more effectiveness: see Andocides *On the Mysteries* 90–91. That this utterance is not peculiar to Athens's domestic policy is attested by many inscriptions, some non-Athenian and some about foreign policy.

oath that Electra is taking—what, as a matter of fact, is an oath to oneself, without divine witnesses? As if the simple proclamation of the unforgetful being were enough to seal the commitment! If it is true that only the oath allows amnesty to overcome resentment, it is because it owes its actuality to the double guarantee that surrounds oath language: that of the gods, invoked as witnesses and ready to punish, and that—especially—of the curse, dreadful machine for punishing perjury that the oath taker unleashes in advance against himself as if it were foreseen that he would repudiate himself. A guarantee more than human is required to prevent the negation from being unmade into denial, and so that no one may dare simply to erase it by subtraction. Magic is required to break the *álaston pénthos*;[62] and to force the *álaston* back on this side of words, politics needs religion.[63]

I shall not forget: I shall not bear resentment. From one utterance to the next, there is all the difference of the ritual of speech, and one hopes it will give the greater actuality to the less-marked of the two sentences.

To conclude, let us try to consider the two ends of the story together.

With each Athenian having sworn for himself, the city expects that the sum of these individual commitments will restore the collectivity; and, on that same occasion, the city shields itself from the conse-quences of perjury, by necessity individual. By thus making sure of the gods' assistance, political authority can establish itself as the censor of memory, alone authorized to decide what is and what must not be the use made of it.

Similarly, the opening of the *Iliad* can invoke no one else than the Muse, because only the daughter of Memory knows how to tell a *mênis* without letting the story be affected by the terrible aura of its object; converting wrath into glory, then, the Muse opens the

---

[62] Nagy, *Comparative Studies,* 258.
[63] See the meaningful remarks of Isocrates in *Against Callimachus* 3 and 23–25.

way of good *anámnēsis,* and the poet is the pure instrument of this transubstantiation.

Restored to its integrity by virtue of the agreement, the community is reestablished and decides. It prohibits any recalling of a litigious past, displaced because contentious, as if Memory appeared in place of Lethe among the dreaded children of Night, as daughter of Strife (Eris). Each Athenian must forget what the *stásis* was if he can, and, whether he can or cannot, each must obey the city by devising for himself a mechanism against the lucid vertigo of *álaston.*

And politics reasserts itself, the civic and reassuring version of the oblivion of misfortunes. Oblivion disappears, erased in amnesty's favor, yet the misfortunes remain. But who would still recall that among the "misfortunes" banned from memory is hidden the very thing that, in the poetical tradition, refused oblivion?

Index Locorum

General Index

MYTH AND POETICS

A Series Edited by

GREGORY NAGY

Helen of Troy and Her Shameless Phantom
by Norman Austin
Poetry in Speech: Orality and Homeric Discourse
by Egbert J. Bakker
The Craft of Poetic Speech in Ancient Greece
by Claude Calame, translated by Janice Orion
Masks of Dionysus
edited by Thomas H. Carpenter and Christopher A. Faraone
The Odyssey *in Athens: Myths of Cultural Origins*
by Erwin F. Cook
The Poetics of Supplication: Homer's Iliad *and* Odyssey
by Kevin Crotty
Poet and Hero in the Persian Book of Kings
by Olga M. Davidson
Gender and Genre in the Folklore of Middle India
by Joyce Burkhalter Flueckiger
The Ravenous Hyenas and the Wounded Sun: Myth and Ritual in Ancient India
by Stephanie W. Jamison
Poetry and Prophecy: The Beginnings of a Literary Tradition
edited by James L. Kugel
The Traffic in Praise: Pindar and the Poetics of Social Economy
by Leslie Kurke
Topographies of Hellenism: Mapping the Homeland
by Artemis Leontis
Mothers in Mourning
by Nicole Loraux, translated by Corinne Pache
Epic Singers and Oral Tradition
by Albert Bates Lord
The Singer Resumes the Tale
by Albert Bates Lord, edited by Mary Louise Lord
The Language of Heroes: Speech and Performance in the Iliad
by Richard P. Martin

Heroic Sagas and Ballads
by Stephen A. Mitchell
The Anger of Achilles: Mênis in Greek Epic
by Leonard Muellner
Greek Mythology and Poetics
by Gregory Nagy
Myth and the Polis
edited by Dora C. Pozzi and John M. Wickersham
*Knowing Words: Wisdom and Cunning in the Classical Traditions of
China and Greece*
by Lisa Raphals
*Heroic Poets, Poetic Heroes: The Ethnography of Performance in an
Arabic Oral Epic Tradition*
by Dwight Fletcher Reynolds
Homer and the Sacred City
by Stephen Scully
Singers, Heroes, and Gods in the Odyssey
by Charles Segal
The Mute Immortals Speak: Pre-Islamic Poetry and the Poetics of Ritual
by Suzanne Pinckney Stetkevych
Phrasikleia: An Anthropology of Reading in Ancient Greece
by Jesper Svenbro, translated by Janet E. Lloyd
The Jewish Novel in the Ancient World
by Lawrence M. Wills

Lightning Source UK Ltd.
Milton Keynes UK
UKHW012046050421
381358UK00011B/227